A SHORT ACCOUNT

OF THE LIVES

OF THE

BISHOPS OF CALCUTTA

D1871213

Owing to the antiquity and rarity of this book, certain pages are regrettably absent, and readability is compromised due to the blurring of the original text. If you possess any insights regarding the availability of these missing sections, kindly inform us. Your assistance is crucial in ensuring the completion of this significant work for the benefit of future generations.

A SHORT ACCOUNT OF THE LIVES OF THE BISHOPS OF CALCUTTA

W CRAWFORD BROMEHEAD

GYAN

Published by

Gyan Publishing House
5, Ansari Road
Daryaganj, New Delhi-110002
Phone: 011-47034999, 9811692060
E-mail: books@gyanbooks.com

Distribution Network
gyanbooks.com
India, USA, Canada, UK, Australia

© Publisher

All rights reserved. No part of this work may be reproduced, stored, adapted, or transmitted in any form or by any means, electronic, mechanical, photocopying, micro-filming, recording or otherwise, or translated in any language, without the prior written permission of the copyright owner and the publisher.

ISBN: 978-93-6920-139-6 (PB)

First Published, 1876

2nd Impression 2025

Printed at: Gyan Press, Delhi.

The book is sold subject to the condition that it shall not, by way of trade or otherwise, be lent, resold, hired out, or otherwise circulated without the prior publisher's written consent.

A SHORT ACCOUNT OF THE LIVES OF THE BISHOPS OF CALCUTTA
Author: W CRAWFORD BROMEHEAD

A SHORT ACCOUNT

OF THE LIVES

OF THE

BISHOPS OF CALCUTTA,

GATHERED FROM THEIR PUBLISHED BIOGRAPHIES
AND FROM OTHER SOURCES;

BY

W. CRAWFORD BROMEHEAD,
Senior Chaplain St. John's, Calcutta.

Calcutta:
W. NEWMAN & CO., 3, DALHOUSIE SQUARE.

1876.

PREFACE.

The following short Memoirs were originally published in the pages of the Indian *Church Gazette*, in the years 1869 and 1870. Some of the remarks interspersed here and there throughout the volume, and having reference to the circumstances of the time, will in consequence now be found somewhat out of date, but instead of re-writing them and so perhaps confusing the style, it has been thought better to leave the remarks as they stand, only asking the reader to remember the date at which they were written.

The excuse which the writer has to offer for bringing back to the light, what would otherwise have been buried in the files of our Diocesan Church Paper, is, that the few facts of which he had after considerable pains and difficulty possessed himself seemed likely to be serviceable to those who wish to know something, however little that something may be, of the History of the See of Calcutta.

It is hoped that this small and unpretentious volume may lead those who can get hold of them to study Le Bas' Life of Middleton, Heber's Life and Journal, Robinson's Last Days of Bishop Heber, James' Brief Memoirs of John Thomas James, Bateman's Life of Daniel Wilson, and Mrs. Cotton's Memoir of George Edward Lynch Cotton.

To all of these the writer is under extensive obligations, as well as to a rare old Book, *The Bengal Obituary*.

Wherever the works above-named have been quoted, the extracts are marked by inverted commas, and it must be understood where these appear in each Memoir that the attention of the reader is particularly directed to the larger and more bulky Biographies.

LIVES
OF
THE BISHOPS OF CALCUTTA.

MIDDLETON.

Thomas Fanshawe Middleton, the first Bishop of Calcutta, was born at Kedleston, Derbyshire, on the 26th of January 1769. He was the only son of his father, who was the rector of the place. He was educated till his 10th year by his parents at home, and he then went on the 21st April 1779 to the Blue Coat School, Christ's Hospital, in London. Here the foundation of his ripe scholarship, and solid attainments was laid, and in gratitude for the benefits he had received there, he transmitted to the Governors, shortly before his death, the sum of £400. From the Blue Coat School, he removed in due time as an exhibitioner to Pembroke College, Cambridge, and in January 1792, he took his B.A. degree, graduating as 4th Senior Optime. In the following March he was ordained Deacon by the Bishop of Lincoln, Dr. Pretyman, as Curate of Gainsborough.

Here he became the editor of a small periodical, called the *Country Spectator*, which, though it did not last more than eight months, served to introduce him to Dr. Pretyman (brother to the Bishop above mentioned), Archdeacon and Precentor of Lincoln, who engaged him as domestic tutor to his sons. In 1793 he removed from Norwich, whither he had gone with the Pretymans, to Tansor, Northamptonshire, to which Dr. Pretyman had presented him ; and in 1797 he married Elizabeth Maddison, a lady of the County of Lincoln. She was of superior attainments, and with her own hand transcribed for the Press most of his publications, especially the Treatise on the use of the Greek article in the New Testament, which laid the foundation of his fame, and stamped him as an erudite and polished scholar of the highest order.

It is much to be regretted that Mr. Kaye, the writer of *Christianity in India*, has taken such a disparaging view of this great work of Dr. Middleton's, as well as of his laborious and most useful career in general. He speaks of the work as if it were a mere grammatical exercise resembling the editing of a Greek play or an oration of Demosthenes, whereas it is really a theological treatise elucidating and bringing into prominence some of the most important doctrines on which our salvation depends.

In 1802, the living of Little Bytham and Castle Bytham was added to that of Tansor, and in 1809 a Prebendal stall at Lincoln was added to these. In 1811, Tansor and the Bythams were exchanged for St. Pancras, London, and Pultenham, Herts, which led in 1812 to the Archdeaconry of Huntingdon. Being now, as Rector of St. Pancras', resident in London, Dr. Middleton became one of the most active and ardent members of the Committee of the Society for Promoting Christian Knowledge.

The editorship of the *British Critic* was undertaken by him about this time, and he was one of the Committee appointed to revise Mant and D'oyley's Commentary on the Bible. In the year 1813, his attention was directed to India by his having to deliver, in the name of the S.P.C.K. a charge to Christophilus Augustinus Jacobi, who was going as a Missionary to the southern part of india.

We now proceed to the period immediately preceding the erection of the first Indian Bishopric. It can hardly be believed now-a-days with what pain and difficulty the battle was won which brought the Gospel free course in India. We may give the opponents of its introduction every credit for sincerity, when they asserted, that its appearance, as represented by a band of Missionaries, or an army of Chaplains, marshalled under a Bishop, would be a signal for a general outbreak which would extend from Cape Comorin to the Himalayas; but we can give them very little credit for penetration, knowledge of the real feelings of the natives, or trust in the God of righteousness, purity and truth. At last, however, so far as preliminaries go, the battle was won. Buchanan, Venn, Wilberforce, and their coadjutors, had managed to get into the New East India Charter of 1813, a clause at the end in favor of Missions, and of the institution of the Bishopric and three Archdeaconries.

And so, on 8th May 1814, Dr. Middleton was consecrated by the Archbishop of Canterbury and the Bishops of Lincoln and Salisbury, Bishop of Calcutta, and on 8th June 1814 he sailed from Portsmouth in the ship *Warren Hastings,* accompanied by Mrs. Middleton, Mr. Loring, Fellow of Magdalen College, Oxford, who had been appointed Archdeacon of Calcutta, Mr. Barnes, Fellow of Exeter College, Oxford, who had been nominated Archdeacon of Bombay, and a young solicitor, Mr. Abbott (father of the late Diocesan Registrar), who was going out to practise in the Supreme Court, and who was to officiate as the Bishop's Secretary. He piled up his cabin with more than 100 vols. Hebrew, Greek, Persian, Latin, French, English; and studied Persian and Hebrew on the voyage.

The only place that he landed at during the whole time was Madeira, where he performed service, and spent several days. He was much struck with the loveliness and rugged beauty of the island. In one of his rambles his clerical dress was remarked upon by the bystanders, one of whom he heard say "What a pity he is a heretic, his perdition is inevitable." The fleet in which he sailed was, through fear of the American privateers, convoyed by the ship *Cumberland* to the latitude of the Cape, where the convoy left them and returned home. At this point the Bombay ships also separated from them, and the Calcutta-bound vessels proceeded by themselves.

At length, after a voyage of more than five mouths, on 28th November 1814, he landed very quietly at Calcutta. No public or official demonstration was made upon his arrival, which rather disappointed him; but his private reception was most gratifying and all that could be wished. On Christmas-day he preached to 1,300 persons and administered the Holy Communion to 160 at St. John's Cathedral. The fears which had been entertained in England about the effects of the Bishop's advent were soon shewn to be utterly futile and absurd. The natives welcomed the Bishop as a friend, and were most anxious, whenever they gained access to him, to shew their good-will and respect. It had been currently said, the Bishop says, by the natives, before his arrival, "You have a head of your army, and a head of your law, and of every department, but your religion!" This reproach was now no longer possible.

It was but however a poor body of clergy that Bishop Middleton was at the head of on his arrival. The roll of chaplains on the list was—

Calcutta	15
Madras	12
Bombay	5
Total ...	32

but of them more than half seem to have been absent or *hors-de-combat*, so that, according to Mr. Abbott, the effective force was :—

Bengal	8
Madras	5 or 6
Bombay	1
Total ...	14 or 15

As a natural consequence, the general state of religion in the country was at a low ebb ; and the Chaplains themselves, through want of episcopal superintendence and encouragement, and from being such isolated units in the midst of a careless mass of military or civil servants of Government, had, in too many instances, entirely forfeited that respect and reverence which is due to their sacred office. Happily there had been and were bright lights among them, such as Buchanan, Henry Martyn, David Brown, Corrie, and a few others, but upon the whole they sadly required elevating and rousing to a sense of their duty.

It was no easy task, therefore, to which the Bishop was set, and it appeared to him as if, while the Armenians, the Roman Catholics, the Scotch Presbyterians and Protestant Dissenters in general, were all active and occupied, the members of the Church of England were doing nothing at all by comparison. In the first hot weather that he went through, the Bishop was a martyr to prickly-heat, of which plague he gives a very graphic and amusing account. He had many other things to vex and annoy him besides this, but he experienced some satisfaction in starting the S. P. C. K. Diocesan Committee, in holding his first Confirmation in July, in regulating the affairs of the Calcutta Free school, in licensing his Chaplains, in enquiring from them as to the general state and condition of his diocese, and in preparing and delivering in the Cathedral of St. John's, his Primary Charge.

In December 1815, a little more than a year after his arrival in Calcutta, Bishop Middleton left on his first Visitation for Madras and Bombay. He arrived at Madras on the eve of Christmas-day. His chief doings there may be summed up by saying that he started an S. P. C. K. Association, strengthened the hands of the Missionaries, presided at a Government School Examination, consecrated the Cathedral of St George, and paid a state visit—the ceremony and splendour of which appears to have impressed him much—to the Nabob of the Carnatic. After a few days' stay at Madras, the Bishop started for the south, and arrived first at the Seven Pagodas,—a group of very interesting ruins and remains, some of them cut out of the native rock, and some of them built of huge stones without mortar, at Mahabalipooram, situated by the sea some thirty-three miles south of Madras.

From the Seven Pagodas he went on to Pondichéry, Cuddalore, Chillumbrum, and Tranquebar. The Danish Missions at Tranquebar were in a very destitute and depressed state, and the Bishop was the means, through the money supplied to him by the S. P. C. K., of saving them from perishing entirely. Thence he went on to Trichinopoly, and entered upon the ground occupied by the saintly Swartz. He visited the Great Temple of Seringham, lying about two miles from Trichinopoly, and built upon a large island in the river Cauvery, with its seven courts, wall within wall, its *choultry* or *sarâi* of a thousand pillars, its costly jewels, and its enormous cyclopean gateway; and then he went down to Tanjore, where was the house in which Swartz chiefly lived, and eventually died. Here he enjoyed the pleasure of meeting the very same Rajah of Tanjore to whom Swartz had acted as tutor, who venerated and loved the apostolic-minded man so much, and erected a costly marble monument to his memory, with the following lines of his own composition incised upon it:—

> " Firm wert thou, humble and wise,
> Honest, pure, and free from disguise;
> Father of orphans, the widows' support,
> Comfort in sorrow of every sort.
> To the benighted dispenser of light,
> Doing and pointing to that which is right;
> Blessing to princes, to people, to me,
> May I, my father, be worthy of thee,
> Wisheth and prayeth thy Sarabojee."

Both at Trichinopoly and at Tanjore the Bishop strengthened the hands of the Missionaries—Mr. Poblé and Mr. Kohlhoff—helped them with handsome donations, and gave them valuable hints for extending and improving their educational and religious efforts. From Tanjore he went on to Palamcottah, the capital of Tinnevelly, but did not stay long there, as the great work which has since taken place in that region was then only in its early dawn. He received, however, deputations from the Native Christians, and noticed with much satisfaction the establishment of several Native Churches of rude and simple materials, put together by their own hands. Hence he crossed the Ghâts not far from Cape Comorin, and entered Cochin.

Here he was first brought into contact with the Syrian Christians in whom he took so deep an interest, and whom he endeavoured, unfortunately without the slightest apparent effect, to lead into the paths of a higher and purer faith. His especial ground of interest in them was, that they were an ancient establishment of the Church who had managed to hold their own, at least to a considerable extent, against the Roman Catholics when the Portuguese dominion was paramount in Malabar. Again and again did he sit for hours with the Syrian Archbishop and his priests, learning from them all about their faith, their ritual, their liturgies, their copies of the Scriptures, the habits of their priesthood, their ecclesiastical ceremony; but although, like Asiatics in general, they were delighted at seeing that the *burra Lat Padre Sahib* (Great Lord Bishop) took such an interest in them; were very civil and complaisant, receiving his presents of books with the greatest gratitude, and professing hopes that perpetual friendship, green and flourishing as the tender shoot, and unfailing as the perennial stream, might subsist between themselves and the Bishop, and all that belonged to him, they still did nothing at all for their improvement or reformation; and when the Bishop three years after re-visited them, hoping that his first visit might have had some good effect, he found them in precisely the same state as before—not one atom, so far as he could judge, either elevated or improved in any way whatsoever.

From Cochin the Bishop sailed for Cannanore, for the purpose of licensing the Church. Archdeacon Loring here left him, and returned *viá* Madras to Calcutta. The Bishop proceeded on his way, and reached Bombay on the 14th

May 1816. Here his first care was to found an Association of the Society for the Promotion of Chritsian Knowledge, and on the 7th July he consecrated the Cathedral under the name of St. Thomas the Apostle of India. The Society for the Education of the Poor received much of his attention, and he preached a sermon, which was afterwards printed on its behalf. He also received several visits from an Armenian Bishop, who had come from Mesopotamia to meet him, and who wished for his help in obtaining some copies of the Scriptures. He visited the Island of Elephanta, and entered with his usual zest into the examination of its wondrous cave monuments. He also spent some time in the Island of Sal-sette at the mouth of the harbour.

On the 17th September 1816, he left Bombay for Goa. He gives a dreary picture of the old town, once the Portuguese capital of Western India. It was, he says, a spectacle melancholy and oppressive to see its grass-grown and deserted streets, and to think that this was once the Lady of European kingdoms in the East.

On the 1st October 1816, he landed once more at Cannanore, and held a confirmation there; thence he again visited Cochin, and spent some time in enquiring into the state and condition of the Colony of Black and White Jews which is found there. These Jews, according to their own account, landed, near the end of the fifth century, at Crunganore, whence they were driven by the Inquisition 300 years since. They harbour strong hopes of returning some day to their own land, and of witnessing the restoration of their own temple at Jerusalem.

After this the Bishop spent some time in visiting the various Syrian churches of Cochin, and eventually embarked on 16th October 1816, and on the 21st arrived at Colombo.

His reception here was cordial and encouraging, and he speaks in the highest terms of the character and conduct of the Governor Sir Thomas Brownrigg. As usual, he suggested the formation of an S. P. C. K. Association, and carried it into effect. He also gave assistance in the extension of missionary enterprise, and wrote home, proposing an Archdeaconry of Colombo, from which the Bishopric in due time sprung. Towards the end of 1816, the Bishop returned to Calcutta.

During this year, 1816, his mind, ever active about education, began to brood over the thought of a Missionary College for all India. The idea seems to have been suggested to him by Mr. Kohlhoff of Tanjore, whose son (now at work near Trichinopoly) was actually educated at Bishop's College. It was, however, several years before the plan began to bear palpable fruit. The want of Chaplains perplexed and distressed him very much ; he was constantly writing for them, but the unavoidable delays in correspondence with England were most aggravating to him. He had much comfort towards the end of the year 1817, in the arrival of a new Domestic Chaplain, Mr. Hawtayne.

The year 1818 was remarkable for a most fatal outbreak of the *cholera morbus.* The Bishop's remarks upon this scourge show the deep interest which he took in the natives, and so do many valuable remarks which are found in his letters of this year's date regarding the Calcutta School Book Society and the Hindoo College, whose influence was just now beginning to be felt, and the establishment of a Diocesan School for the benefit of the natives in the southern suburbs of the city. In this year also, on 8th August, he laid the foundation of the Church at Dum-Dum. But his most remarkable effort during the course of the year was his draft of the plan of his proposed Mission College, at which he laboured so steadily and unceasingly till his death. After despatching his letter home upon this subject, and having delivered at the commencement of 1819 his second Charge, the Bishop started on his second Visitation.

He first went to Madras, strengthened the Vepery Mission at that place, held a confirmation, and then sailed for Penang. His stay there did not extend over many days, but it sufficed for him to establish an Association for the S.P.C.K., to preach, confirm and strengthen the hearts of the brethren in those parts. Towards the end of May 1819, he returned to Calcutta. Before his return to Calcutta he set at work to build a National Day School, and a Church for the benefit of the poor in the suburbs. This was the origin of the St. James' Church and School, now the Calcutta Boys' School—both of them lately revived so happily by the exertions of Archdeacon Pratt. In this year Archdeacon Mousley of Madras died, whose character the Bishop thus describes :—" He was one of the most amiable men I have known, a jealous and conscientious churchman, a scholar, and a gentleman, and so much beloved and respected that great deference was paid to him, even by those who differed from him in certain points." Mr. Edward Vaughan, the Senior Chaplain at Madras, was appointed by the Bishop as his successor.

In this year the Cingalese and Tamil Common Prayer-books were printed by the S.P.C.K., and a large grant of books sent at Mr. Marsden's (the Chaplain of New South Wales) request to Australia.

The Bishop's sight about this period seems to have been failing, as he speaks of being unable to read by candle-light. One of his Chaplains, Mr. Fisher, having been reported by some military authority for tampering with his men, one of whom had been converted to Christianity, the Bishop had the pleasure of receiving from Mr. Fisher a most satisfactory and ample vindication of himself and his convert, which gave him much satisfaction, and overwhelmed the military man with confusion.

In the year 1820 we find the Bishop catechising the children during Lent at the Cathedral every Wednesday, and preaching on the Fridays to very considerable congregations; going on with his plans for his Mission College constantly, and attending the Committees of the Free School. It may strike us as strange that he never went up-country; he himself says he was constantly asked when he should go to the Upper Provinces—to Agra and Delhi? But, he says, till the Company will build Churches in those parts, I should be able to effect but little, and even then I know not how I could find time.

At length, on the 15th December 1820, the Bishop had the inexpressible joy of laying, with his own hands, the foundation-stone of Bishop's College.

It may be allowed that the benefit of the College has not as yet come up to the Bishop's expectations. Its position is against it, and it is rather too large an institution for a mere Missionary College, unless it could be made to include the whole of India, which, since the establishment of Bishoprics in Madras, Ceylon, and Bombay, it unfortunately has not done. Still, however, it cannot be said to have existed in vain. Several of the most valuable and effective of our Missionary labourers at this moment were trained in it, and it must ever remain, as long as the Church of England exists in this land, an essential to the Diocese.

In 1821, the Bishop proceeded in his Visitation to Bombay, preached before the Society for the Education of the Poor, and carried on other good works. While here he heard that his name had been mentioned at home in evidence before the House of Lords as having been present at a *nautch*; he instantly wrote to contradict and explain the statement. It arose in reference to Queen Caroline's having been at an entertainment when some kind of indecent dance had been performed by an Oriental, and one of the witnesses on the Queen's side said there could be no harm in Oriental dances because the Bishop of Calcutta had been present at a *nautch* at the Governor-General's. The Bishop, however, had not been there, and so was able to deny the charge so far as he himself went; but unfortunately Mrs. Middleton had been there with some other ladies who were staying with her at the time. However, the matter may be regarded as rather a joke than anything else; for it is not likely that the Governor-General would allow an indecent *nautch* at his house; but it shows that Bishops' wives should be careful where they go and what they do. The Bishop called at Cochin, and at Colombo on his return voyage. At Colombo a grand Cathedral was built of bamboos and palm leaves, and was to have been lighted up in the Bishop's honor at night, but unfortunately a tropical storm came on and strewed the Cathedral in ruins.

In June 1821, the Bishop returned to Calcutta. He found Dr. Mill and Mr. Alt, the Principal and Professor of Bishop's College, had arrived in February, but could not yet be set to work because the College was not ready. In this year the Bishop held his third Visitation, and delivered his third Charge. All his Charges aimed chiefly at reducing his Diocese to discipline and order—at impressing upon his clergy a sense of their high calling—at the evolution of wise plans for the spread of genuine Christianity among professing Christians, for the diffusion of education, and for the conversion of the heathen. Like all his writings, they are models of classical composition, and run, from end to end, in measured and dignified language, which betokens the thorough scholar and the clear-headed man. In a letter which he writes to Mr. Norris on 1st January 1821, we find a memo, that on the 20th November, he gave full seven hours to the examination of the boys of the Free School. This is a fact that in itself speaks volumes for the man, and shows that he was in education at least an enthusiast.

Wishing to reduce his diocese, as much as possible, to an English standard, the Bishop was very anxious for the establishment of an Ecclesiastical Court. He met with some opposition in regard to this, especially from the Chief Justice at Madras; but the Court, called the Consistorial Court, was duly set on foot, though it does not appear to have been of much practical use.

We now approach the closing scene of his life. The paucity of his Chaplains and the difficulties of his position in endeavouring to reduce his diocese to order, seem to have preyed upon his mind, and irritated him so much that he got into a nervous feverish state, which was calculated, in case of any slight accident, to pass into some kind of dangerous disease, which, as the following extract (from Le Bas' Life of Bishop Middleton) will show was not long in developing itself:—

"On the Monday preceding his death he received the clergy, as was his custom, at dinner. In the early part of the evening he was severely agitated by some information respecting certain proceedings which had been instituted against him in the Supreme Court by one of his own clergy, on whom he had been under the necessity of inflicting censure. This depression, however, he shook off, and became unusually cheerful and animated, and exhibited with much appearance of satisfaction some handsome improvements which he had recently made in his residence. On Tuesday, July 2nd, he unfortunately persisted in visiting the College at an early hour, in the afternoon, in spite of the remonstrances of his physician. * * * *

"On the Wednesday he was occupied for 8 hours together in writing to Government respecting the proceedings in the Supreme Court above alluded to. He then declared that he was quite exhausted, and proposed to Mrs. Middleton, who had been suffering from ill-health, that she should accompany him in the carriage before the sun was gone down. They had not proceeded far when the slant sun, which is always dangerous, and especially at the damp and sickly season of the year, shone full upon him. This slight cause acting upon a shattered frame of nerves was sufficient to produce fatal effects. He immediately declared that he was struck by the sun, and returned home. On retiring to rest he said he thought himself seriously ill, and that he knew not what would be the consequence. He nevertheless positively refused to call in medical advice. In the course of the evening his symptoms became aggravated to an alarming degree, and indicated the presence of a fever of a type and character scarcely known in England, and very rare even in India. The high pulse, hot skin, and other ordinary symptoms, were present only in a very slight degree, neither were they prevalent in any considerable extent during his illness. But there appeared from the very first a most distressing anxiety, irritability and restlessness which it was impossible to subdue, and which made his illness doubly painful to his family and his friends. He repeatedly insisted on getting up to write, and it was not without the greatest difficulty that he was restrained from actually doing so. All this while he strictly forbade Mrs. Middleton to send for a physician, till at last on Thursday the fever had become so violent that he was prevailed to call in Dr. Nicolson. * * He was now perhaps fully conscious of his danger, still it seems he would not allow any intimation of his alarming condition to be conveyed to his friends. * * In the course of the following Monday there were slight appearances of amendment. Some hopes were even entertained that the danger was passing by, and that a favorable crisis might be at hand; but these were soon dissipated by an alarming accession of fever and irritability which came on towards the evening. He then quitted his library, and walked incessantly up and down his drawing-room in a state of the most appalling agitation. About 9 o'clock his Chaplain, Mr. Hawtayne, was admitted to see him, and was inexpressibly shocked to find him on his couch in a state, to all appearance, of violent delirium; his thougths wandering, his articulation gone, his faculties, in short, a melancholy wreck at the mercy of the tempest which had shattered them. In that condition he lay breathing and struggling violently till a short time previous to his departure. The severity of the conflict, then appeared wholly to cease—a smile of unspeakable serenity and peace spread itself over his features, and in a few minutes, he gently expired. Such was the tranquillity of the last moment, that it was not marked by a struggle or even a movement."

Thus passed away at the age of 54 years India's first Bishop having fought a good fight against many difficulties, and having done much to determine the shape which the Church in India should hereafter assume. In many respects he was just the man required for the occasion. He brought order out of chaos, and laid the foundation of the Indian Church's laws and principles. He has been accused of being a formalist and a slave of routine, but if there is any truth in the accusation it can never be said that he laid on other men's shoulders burdens which he would not bear himself. It was because he was persuaded that law and order were primitive and apostolical that he enforced them, not to add to his own importance or to increase his individual power.

The Bishop in his will directed that his remains should be interred in the vault under the Chapel of Bishop's College if it were consecrated, and left the following inscription to be carved on a tablet in the Chapel :—

Prope hunc locum
Mortales exuvias reponendas volui

Or in case the Chapel might be incomplete—

In hoc sacello
Nomen meum servandum volui
THOMAS FANSHAW MIDDLETON, S.T.P.
Primus Diœceseos Calcuttensis Episcopus
Hujusce Collegii Ædificandi suasor
Et pro viribus adjutor
Jesu Christe.
Lux mundi peccatorum salus
præconibus tuis hinc exeuntibus,
Optima quæque dona elargiaris
Et miserescas animæ meæ.

Obiit Anno Redemptoris, MDCCCXXII, Ætatis LIV, Episcopatus IX.
Voluit Elizabetha uxor conjunctissima eodem marmore insigniri.

This inscription may now be seen on the east wall of Bishop's College Chapel.

He was buried at the east end of St. John's Church, where a black marble slab marks his last resting place, incised—

LIVES

OF

THE BISHOPS OF CALCUTTA.

HEBER.

Reginald Heber, the second Bishop of Calcutta, was born on 21st April 1783, at Malpas, in the country of Chester, where his father was for many years co-Rector. The family of Hebers or Hayber, as it appears to have been formerly written, was of considerable antiquity in the county of York, and is supposed to have derived its name from a hill in Craven, called Hayber or Haybergh. His early childhood was distinguished by mildness of disposition, parental obedience, consideration for the feelings of those around him, and that trust in Providence which formed through life such a prominent feature in his character. When little more than two years of age, he was dangerously ill with whooping-cough, for which he was (according to the barbarous and ignorant medical practice of the day) ordered to be bled. His mother took him on her knees, and said—"Dr. Currie wishes you to lose a little blood. I hope you will not object." His answer was—"I will do whatever you please, mamma." On the nurse screaming out that they were going to murder her child, "Poor Jane," he said, "let her go down stairs." When the apothecary took hold of his arm, he exclaimed "Do not hold me;" and when told that if he moved he would be hurt, "I won't stir," he said, and held out his arm, steadily looking all the time at the course of the operation. The following year, when travelling with his parents on a very stormy day across the mountainous country between Ripon and Craven, his mother was much alarmed, and proposed to leave the carriage and walk. Reginald, sitting on her knees, said—"Do not be afraid, mamma, God will take care of us." He was very patient whenever ill, and during his infancy he was much afflicted with inflammatory disorders. He also displayed from the earliest years a retentive and accurate memory, and great thirst for knowledge. At six years of age, on recovering from an attack of typhus fever, his first request was to be allowed to learn his Latin Grammar, that he might have employment while lying in bed.

He could read the Bible fluently when five years old, and on one occasion, when his father and a friend were discussing the point of where a particular passage was, his father on his coming into the room referred the matter to him, and he at once named chapter and verse correctly. At the age of about seven, a party of his young companions were amusing themselves with Scripture riddles and questions, and on the question being sportively asked "Where was Moses when the candle went out?" Reginald said "On Mount Nebo, for it was there that his lamp of life went out." He was often observed on his knees in his own room when he thought no one saw him. Thus it might be truly said of him that from a child he knew the Holy Scriptures, and carried out their sound lessons practically. He was fond of drawing and of natural history, and was always remarkable for his keen powers of observation. When a squirrel was given to his little sister as a plaything, he could not bear to see it in a cage, and he persuaded her to take it to a tree, and let it go, that she might see how happy it was at being set at liberty. He was of an absent, contemplative, and inquisitive turn, and was very fond of asking questions, but never in a rude or awkward way. He read rapidly, and took in a page of a book almost at a glance. His father, who was a good classical scholar, bought him the rudiments of the classics, and his proficiency was so rapid that at the age of seven he had turned the Fables of Phædrus into English verse.

The following year, 1791, he was placed at the Grammar School of Whitchurch under Dr. Kent, and an instance of his intense powers of abstraction is mentioned in that he was wrapped up in a book during a noisy "Barring out," and never knew what was being done for two hours till the increasing darkness obliged him to lay down his book. In 1796, at the age of thirteen, he was placed under Mr. Bristow, a clergyman, who took twelve pupils, at Neasdon, near London, and here he met his greatest friend in after-life, John Thornton, eldest son of Samuel Thornton, late the M.P., for Surrey. He was so unselfish and kind to the poor, that when he was sent to the school his mother used to sew the banknotes she gave him into his trouser pockets, lest he should give them away on the road.

The following instance will show how he attempted to illustrate his own experience of what he read in books. He had just been reading how one of our African travellers had successfully parried the attack of a wild bull by holding his hat before his face, and gesticulating in such a manner as to frighten the animal and make him run away. There happened to be a savage bull in a field close by, so Reginald went towards him acting exactly as the African traveller had done, and expecting a similar result; but instead of running away the bull furiously rushed at him, and he only escaped by jumping over some rails into a garden close by. On the other side of the rails was a pond, along the edge of which Reginald, after clearing the fence, ran, but the bull could not turn so sharp, and in the ardour of pursuit went right into the water, and, after floundering about for some time, stuck in the mud on the opposite side.

At the age of seventeen (A.D. 1800), we find him talking about going up to Oxford, and in November of that year he went up to Brasenose. There is no appearance in his letters about this time of any tendency to scepticism or juvenile licence of any kind. All that we find is a jubilant tone connected with high spirits and playfulness of mind, but there is not the slightest appearance of anything like vice or excess; on the contrary, though his reading was varied and extensive, it was evidently regulated by the strictest propriety and religious principle. His manner is described by a friend about this time as generally free and natural, but at times when high subjects are introduced, a species of inspiration seems to seize him, and he pours out a store of learning, research, and varied information in such a manner as to wrap all hearers in astonishment and wonder. In conversation he had a habit of not looking up at his hearers.

Some of the Oxford customs—the procession of the Mallard on the roof of All Souls' with lighted torches, of the Boar's head at Queen's, and other remnants of what he calls Gothicism—seem to have struck him as useful in their way in keeping up a reverence for traditional customs of hoar antiquity. By far the most striking event in Heber's college career was the recitation of his Seatonian Prize Poem "Palestine" in the Sheldonian Theatre at the Annual Oxford Commemoration in 1803. The effect which the recitation produced is well described in the following lines by a Miss Jermyn:—

"Hushed was the busy hum, nor voice nor sound
Through the vast concourse marked the moment near;
A deep and holy silence breath'd around,
And mute attention fixed the listening ear.

When from the *rostrum* burst the hallowed strain,
And Heber kindling with poetic fire,
Stood midst the gazing and expectant train,
And woke to eloquence his sacred lyre.

The youthful student with emphatic tone,
(His lofty subject on his mind impressed)
With grace and energy unrivalled shone,
And roused devotion in each thoughtless breast.

He sang of Palestine—that Holy Land,
Where saints and martyrs and the warrior brave
The cross in triumph planting on its strand,
Beneath its banners sought a glorious grave.

He sang of Calvary—of his Saviour sang
Of the rich mercies of Redeeming Love.
When thro' the crowd spontaneous plaudits rang,
Breathing a foretaste of rewards above.

What means that stifled sob that groan of joy?
Why fall those tears upon the furrowed cheek?
The aged father hears his darling boy;
And, sobs and tears alone *his* feelings speak.

From his full heart the tide of rapture flows,
In vain to stem its rapid course he tries;
He hears the applauding shouts, the solemn close,
And, sinking from excess of joy, he dies."

The two last stanzas allude to a report that when Heber's father heard the reception which his son met with, he was so overcome with joy, that, having been for some time in a weak state of health, the excitement proved too much for him, and he literally died of joy. This was not the fact, at least at the time, though he really did die shortly after. When Heber got free of the crowd who pressed around him with the warmest congratulations, he went straight into his chamber, and was found there by his mother on his knees thanking God that he had been privileged to bestow upon his parents upon that day so much happiness and pleasure.

On 22nd February 1804, his father died at Malpas. He was present; and joined in the last communion, of which, with all its affecting attendant circumstances, he sent a full account to his friend Thornton immediately afterwards. In the course of the same year he took his degree displaying no great proficiency in logic or the exact sciences, but distinguishing himself highly in classical oratory and poetry. He was now 21 years of age, and having still two years to wait before he could take orders, he occupied part of the time by a tour with his friend John Thornton to the north of Europe through Russia, the Crimea, Hungary, Austria, Prussia, and Germany.

It is impossible to give more than a glance here and there at this part of his life. Wherever he goes he observes keenly, and remarks amusingly and illustrates happily, and succeeds in giving an excellent idea of the manners, morals, and general condition of the countries and peoples with which he comes into contact. Norway and Sweden were the first countries visited. Of the Norse peasantry he says:— "The condition of the peasantry is easy; their daily pay for labor is equal to 2*s.* of our money. Wolf-hunting is a very common amusement in winter; the party go out in sledges having a little pig in each sledge, on whose tail they tread to make it squeak, the wolves immediately come out in such numbers that even a good shot is sometimes in danger." He relates how at Christiansund the grass is so short and scanty that the cows are fed on stinking salmon. How the Finnish preachers shout so loud in their sermons that they may be heard in summer when their church-windows are open a full verst off. How the children of the Foundling Asylum at St. Petersburgh used to be suckled by goats; how ice never thaws more than four feet under ground at St. Petersburgh, and is used with advantage in some cases as a foundation to bridges, and other large and heavy piles of architecture. How the chambers occupied by the Emperor Paul, and where he was murdered, are expressly forbidden to be shown. How the women wash clothes at Petersburgh standing for hours on the ice, and plunging their bare arms into the freezing water in 18 or 20 degrees of frost. How after a certain solemn service at one of the Royal Chapels, when the Bishop had given the final blessing, the beautiful young empress came forward and kissed the Bishop's hand, which he returned on her hand and cheek, and how his example was followed by the whole tribe of ecclesiastics "as dirty a race of monks as ever ate salt fish." How, in every Russian cottage, which is always built of logs and moss, two-thirds of the upper-storey are taken up with the principal room, and the remainder is divided between a closet where they cook their victuals and an immense stove, the top of which serves for a favorite sitting and sleeping place, though it was so hot that an Englishman could scarcely bear to lay his hand on it. How they witnessed a wolf burnt on the Volga when a boxed-up wolf was turned out on the ice, and after being baited by dogs and chased by men with *knouts*, and half-worried and beaten to death, was again boxed up for another day's tormentations.

Heber returns from the Continent in September 1806, at the time of a general election, and was seen in the thick of an election contest in favor of his elder brother. He was received by the peasantry at Hodnet with every demonstration of joy, and immediately sat down to prepare himself for the reception of Holy Orders, which he entered upon in 1807, and was instituted by his brother to the family living of Hodnet in Shropshire; soon after which he returned to Oxford to take his degree of M.A. The only dissenters that he had in Hodnet were Methodists, and they were not very numerous, nor did they manage to increase or gain ground while Heber was incumbent. He applied himself sedulously to all parochial duties, visiting the sick and poor, keeping up the school, and preaching steadily three sermons a week. His leisure time he occupied in writing for the *Reviews*, giving preference to the *Quarterly*, in compiling a Hymn-book with the assistance especially of Dean Milman who wrote several of the most beautiful hymns which the volume contains. There were also many gathered from older Hymn Books already in use. The gems of the collection, however, were by Heber himself, and some of these have passed into almost every Hymn Book which has been published since. In 1809 he finished and sent to the press a Poem which he had commenced at Dresden on a sleepless night in 1806. One line in these recent events has turned into a prophecy—

"Spain the brave the virtuous shall be free."

Of course the allusion is to the tyranny of the French, but there is a tyranny over the soul far worse than the French domination, from which Spain seems now to be hopefully rising, and which she needs all our prayers to enable her to consummate happily.

In April 1809, Heber married Amelia, youngest daughter of William Davis Shiply, late Dean of St. Asaph, and granddaughter of the late Jonathan Shiply, Bishop of St. Asaph. The first present that he ever made her was a Bible. It was soon after his marriage that he commenced the composition of the Hymn-book to which we have already alluded. The hymns first appeared in a periodical called the *Christian Observer* in 1811-12. In 1812, Heber commenced a Dictionary of the Bible which formed a favorite object of interest to him in leisure hours for many years after, but it does not appear to have been published. In 1812, the old rectory-house at Hodnet was pulled down, and for the next two years he resided at Moreton, a perpetual Curacy and Chapel of Ease to Hodnet. About this time he was much afflicted with erysipelas, and was obliged to go to Harrowgate for long periods at a time, nor did he succeed in shaking off his malady, except after a long course of hygienics and mercury.

In 1813, a Prebendary of Durham was offered to him, but declined. His letters to friends on Lay Baptism and on the Church of Rome, written about this time, are full of research, piety, and wisdom, and when we see how well and convincingly he can write on such topics when he gave his mind to them, we can scarcely help regretting that he had not leisure among his multifarious occupations, and far-extended travels, to occupy himself with some thing like regular and standard treatises upon the controverted points of orthodox doctrine; but we may well be thankful for what we have got, for it may certainly be said that, as a journal-writer or itinerarian, Heber is without a rival in any age or time. His observation is so keen, his style so cheerful and refreshing, his power of illustration so vivid, and his moralizations so happy and telling.

In 1814, the new rectory-house being completed, Heber returned to Hodnet. His art in instructing the young is evinced by the following anecdote:—"A child, by her mother's request, had been repeating her lesson to him. After listening to the little girl, he gradually began to talk to her on the subject it related to, and when she was asked how she liked saying her lesson to Mr. Heber, she answered, 'Oh very much, and he told me a great many things, but I do not think he knows much more than I do!'" In 1816, he lost his youngest brother, Thomas Cuthbert. He died after a short illness from the rupture of a blood-vessel on the brain; from this period it was usual with him to consecrate every domestic occurrence with a short prayer, which was generally in Latin.

In 1817, the late Bishop of St. Asaph, Dr. Luxmore, appointed Mr. Heber to a stall in the Cathedral at the request of his father-in-law. His journeys into Wales became, in consequence, more frequent, and he usually made them on horseback, beguiling the loneliness of his journeys by poetical compositions of which throughout his life he was so fond. The following may be given as a specimen of them; one is entitled—

"THE SPRING JOURNEY.

"Oh! green was the corn as I rode on my way,
And bright was the dew in the blossoms of May;
And dark was the sycomore's shade to behold,
And the oak's tender leaf was of emerald and gold.

2.

"The thrush from his holly, the lark from his cloud,
Their chorus of rapture sung jovial and loud;
From the soft vernal sky to the soft grassy ground,
There was beauty above me, beneath, and around.

3.

"The mild southern breeze brought a shower from the hill,
And yet tho' it left me all dripping and chill,
I felt a new pleasure as onward I sped.
To gaze where the rainbow gleamed broad overhead.

4.

"O such be life's journey, and such be our skill,
To lose in its blessings the sense of it's ill:
Through sunshine and shower may our progress be even,
And our tears add a charm to the prospect of Heaven."

In July 1818, he thus wrote to his friend R. J. Willmot:— "During the few days I was in Shropshire, I heard a good deal of the New Zealand warriors who had been brought over by a Missionary Society, and were staying with a clergyman in Shropshire. Some roasted rabbits were on the table which he supposed to be cats. On being asked whether New Zealanders eat cats, he answered, 'New Zealander *eatee* hog, him *eatee* dog, him *eatee* rat, him *eatee* creeper (biting his own arm like a dog in search of a flea), him *eatee* warrior and old woman, but him no *eatee* puss."

About this time he was much interested in a movement for reuniting the two great Church of England Missionary Societies—S.P.G. and C.M.S.—under one management, and drew up some rules to that end. The movement came to nothing.

In 1818, he lost his little daughter. In the hymn "Thou art gone to the grave," may be traced the feelings occasioned by this event.

In 1819, on the occasion of a Royal letter for S. P. G., he wrote at St. Asaph the hymn from "Greenland's Icy Mountains," which was first sung in that beautiful Church. His critique on Scott the Annotator's "Force of Truth," written in the same year, is an able and admirable paper. In the course of it he declared himself a decided Anti-Calvinist. It concludes with the following weighty words:— "Do not expect too much certainty on topics which have exercised the sagacity of men from many ages, without any agreement being produced among them, but if you still find perplexities beyond your power, dismiss them from your mind as things which cannot concern you. Secret things belong unto the Lord our God, but in the necessity of an atonement, in justification by faith, and in the obligation which lies on us to work out, with fear and trembling, the salvation thus begun in us, no real difficulties exist, and by these in every system, our entrance to heaven is secured."

In 1820, an epidemic of putrid sorethroat raged at Hodnet. Heber through constant visiting caught the malady. Soon after his recovery, on Good Friday, 1820, he writes—"Preached and administered the Sacrament. I have resolved this day, by God's help, to be more diligent in prayer, to rise earlier, to be more industrious in my studies, to keep a more watchful guard on my temper, to be more diligent in my parochial duties; God help and strengthen me." About this time he engaged for Duncan & Co., to write a life of Jeremy Taylor, and he mentions a fact we never saw elsewhere, that he married a natural daughter of Charles I. He also was employed as a reviewer of Southey's Life of Wesley for the *Quarterly.*

In 1822, he became a candidate for the preachership at Lincoln's Inn, and though he had no particular interest, he gained the post without much difficulty.

On the erection of Calcutta into a See, and on the appointment of Bishop Middleton to the post, Heber's interest in India had been much increased; and he often traced on the map long journeys through the land, which he afterwards visited, while he followed out the course of the labors of Calcutta's primary Bishop. On the death of Bishop Middleton in 1822, Heber's friend, the Hon'ble Mr. Watkin Wynn, wrote at once and offered him the Bishopric. At first he declined it for family reasons, fearing the separations from wife and children which he knew it would occasion, as well as the health of his children, and the being parted from his aged mother; but his wife being of opinion that he ought to accept it, and his own inclination being quite in favor of the glowing East, he, after twice declining it, agreed to go out, saying, "the peace of mind which he felt when he had come to the determination, convinced him that he had done right."

On 22nd April 1823, he took leave of Shropshire. The University of Oxford gave him his D.D., by diploma, as a token of respect, and, on the 18th May, he preached his last sermon in Lincoln's Inn, on the Atonement, on which occasion Mr. Butterworth, a noted Wesleyan, having heard him, remarked, "Thank God for that man; thank God for that man!"

On 1st June 1823, he was consecrated at Lambeth. On 13th June he received the S.P.C.K. valedictory address at Bartlett's buildings, and, on the 16th June, he sailed, with his family, for India. He made several sketches of the Southern Coast; in passing under one part of which he wrote the following quotation:—

> "And we must have danger, and fever, and pain,
> Ere we look on the white rocks of Albion again."

He arranged to have evening prayers on board regularly. On July 3rd, they were off Madeira, where they did not land. On July 26th, the line was crossed, and the usual mummeries were practised. On 19th August, the Cape was passed; on 27th September they sighted the Pagoda of Juggernath. On the 30th, when off False Point, he was roused by a cry which he took to be the "Baby is over board" and he ran out taking off his coat and waistcoat to spring in and try to save his child. The cry, it turned out, was really "Davy is overboard," a seaman named really "Gowen," but supposed to be Davie, having been knocked into the sea by an apprentice lad who had fallen from the mizen gaff. The seaman was saved, but the apprentice boy sunk to rise no more. On 1st October, the pilot was taken on board, and the ship anchored in the Saugor roads. The river at this point, he says, reminded him of the Don between Tcherkast and Asoph.

On the 9th October, they left Diamond Harbour, and went up the river with a light breeze. On 10th October, they left the vessel and proceeded in two boats up the stream. At a distance of about nine miles from the place where they started in boats, they landed among some tall bamboos, and walked nearly a quarter mile to the front of a dingy, deserted-looking house, not very unlike a country gentleman's house in Russia, near some *powder mills.* Here they found carriages waiting for them "drawn by small horses with switch tails," and driven by postillions with whiskers, turbans, bare legs and arms, and jackets with tawdry yellow lace.

All the various objects which strike any one newly arrived in Calcutta, are described in Heber's journal with the utmost truthfulness and with his usual inimitable and sprightly grace. We exclaim involuntarily when we see how his eye catches up every object and his pen so vividly paints it "*Nihil intactum reliquit, nihil quod tetigit non ornavit.*" Government House in Fort William, which he describes as "a large and very handsome building in the centre of the Fort and of the vast square formed by its barracks and other buildings" was placed by the Governor-General, Lord Amherst, at his disposal, and here he went through the ceremony of being introduced to a "considerable number of his clergy," and to an army of "Chobdars,* Sotaburdars, Hurkarus, his Khansamah†, Abdar‡, Sherabdar||, Khitmutgars¶, Sircar**, Sirdar-bearer†† and bearers, *cum multis aliis.*" The number of these "hangers-on" evidently entertained him very much as the following extract shews: "We walked," he says "some time round the square (in the Fort), and were amused to see our little girl walking with her nurse, in great delight at the animals (the *adjutants*) around her, but rather encumbered with the number of servants who had attached themselves to her. For her especial service, a bearer, a khitmutgar, a hurkaru, and a cook, were appointed, and there were, besides the two former, one of the silver-sticks with her, and another bearer with a monstrous umbrella on a long bamboo pole in the manner represented in Chinese screens. My wife soon reduced her nursery establishment; but we afterwards found that it is the custom in Calcutta to go to great expense in the equipage of children."

On the 11th October 1823, he was introduced to Lord Amherst, and afterwards went to the Cathedral (St. John's) where he was installed. On the 28th of October, he paid a visit to Barrackpore, where he was Lord Amherst's guest at Government House, which, he remarks, enjoys a fine view of the river and of the Danish Settlement of Serampore, and is a handsome building containing three fine sitting-rooms, though but few bed-chambers, so that the Aides-de-camp and visitors sleep in bungalows (a corruption of Bengalee) built at a little distance from it in the park.

* Men who carry silver-sticks before people of rank, or messengers, all bearing the generic name of Peons.

† Steward. ‡ Water-cooler. || Butler.

¶ Footmen. ** Agent.

†† Head of all the bearers and *valet-de-chambre.*

On the 4th November 1823, he consecrated the church at Dum-Dum, which he describes as a "military village, the principal European artillery cantonment in India;" and on 12th of the same month (Old) St. James' Church, situate in St. James' Square, south of Boitakhannah, "in the centre of the poorest and most numerous Christian population of Calcutta." "A great many sailors," he says, "come to this church." It fell down in the year 1858, and was replaced by the new St. James' in Circular Road, of which the foundation-stone was laid on 7th June 1862.

About the 18th November 1823, he paid his first visit to the Free School, attending first the Governors' meeting, and then going over the whole institution. He describes its character as it exists now most correctly, except that he says, "There are one or two Hindoos, who are allowed to attend, and who also stand on one side when the catechism is repeated, though they say the Lord's Prayer and read the Scriptures without scruple." There are no Hindoos allowed in the school now, and the number of children stated by Heber at 247 is now about 300.

On 20th November he went with Lady Amherst to visit the Botanical Gardens, which were then under the management of the enthusiastic Botanist, by birth a Dane, Dr. Wallich. "Dr. Wallich," he says, "has the management of another extensive public establishment at Tittaghur, near Barrackpore, of the same nature with this, but appropriated to the introduction of useful plants into Bengal." On the 12th December he attended an examination of the children of Mrs. Wilson's Native Female Schools. On the 25th, Christmas Day, he had 300 communicants at the Cathedral (St. John's) and a large congregation.

During the next few days he took a trip up the river as far as Chandernagore, calling at all the principal places on the way. At Chandernagore he witnessed the presenting of the Christmas *boxes* ("a corruption," he says, "apparently of *bucksheesh*") from the natives to their superiors, of fruit, game, fish, pastry, and sweetmeats.

On the 8th January 1824, he went for a stay of two months to Dr. Wallich's house at Tittaghur on the banks of the river, about two miles from Barrackpore, and in the middle of the Company's Experimental Botanic Garden. About this time, returning one day from Calcutta, he passed a *Suttee*, which had been just consummated. He visited the spot from which foul and stinking odours still exhaled, and could only express his regret at not having arrived two hours sooner so as to have attempted to save the victim's life.

Dr. Marshman, the Baptist Missionary from Serampore, dined with him a day or two afterwards at Tittaghur. Dr. Carey also was asked, but was too lame to go out. He discussed with Marshman the question of the legal abolition of *Suttee*, and found him of the opinion, which afterwards proved to be correct, that it could be abolished without any fear of general public dissatisfaction or popular outbreak. In describing a visit which he paid during February 1824 to Mr. Shakespeare's Rope Bridge Manufactory at Cossipore, he gives the following account of the origin of the name of the River Kurumnasa, over which a rope-bridge had lately been stretched. The name, he says, means "the destroyer of good works," from the circumstance that "an ancient devotee, whose penances, like those of Kehama, had exalted him to Indra's Heaven, having been precipitated headlong by Siva, till his penances broke his fall half-way, directly over the stream in question. He now hangs in the air head downwards, and his saliva flows into and pollutes the water in such a manner that any person who bathes in or even touches it loses the merits of all his antecedent penances, alms, and other acts of piety, reserving however the full benefit of his misdeeds of whatever description."

On April 9th, 1824, he witnessed the *Kali* Festival of the *Churruck* Pooja. Both he and Mrs. Heber seem to have visited the swinging-places in the *maidan* and Boitakhannah, and to have seen the devotees swing round. On the 15th June, he left Calcutta on his Visitation of the Upper Provinces for Dacca. He was obliged to leave Mrs. Heber, with her infant child, behind. Mr. Stowe accompanied him as his Domestic Chaplain. The Corries, also on their way to Bhaugulpore, started at the same time. At the mouth of the Jellinghy he parted from the Corries; and, on the 4th July 1824, he was at Dacca, where he preached to a small congregation in a very small but pretty Gothic church, Mr. Parish the Chaplain reading prayers. Here he had the great grief of losing his Domestic Chaplain, Mr. Stowe, who died of dysentery. Having exchanged visits attended with considerable state with the Nawab, and having consecrated the church and burial ground, and administered the rite of Confirmation, he left Dacca on the morning of July 12th. At Furreedpore he received news from Mrs. Heber of the dangerous illness of both their infant children, which made him at first inclined to hurry home to Calcutta, but preferring his public to his private duty, he resolved to continue his Visitation, and proceeded on his way hoping to meet Mrs. Heber in Bombay. His thoughts at this time are expressed in the following lines to his wife:—

"If thou wert by my side, love,
  How fast would evening fail
In green Bengala's palmy grove,
  Listening the nightingale.

"If thou, my love, wert by my side
  My babies at my knee,
How gaily would our pinnace glide
  O'er Gunga's mimic sea.

"I miss thee at the dawning grey,
  When, on our deck reclined,
In careless ease my limbs I lay,
  And woo the cooler wind.

"I miss thee when, by Gunga's stream,
  My twilight steps I guide;
But most beneath the lamp's pale beam
  I miss thee from my side.

"I spread my books, my pencil try
  The lingering morn to cheer;
But miss thy kind, approving eye,
  Thy meek, attentive ear.

"But when of morn and eve the star
  Beholds me on my knee,
I feel, tho' thou art distant far,
  Thy prayers ascend for me.

"Then on! then on! where duty leads;
  My course be onward still:
O'er broad Hindoostan's sultry mead—
  O'er bleak Almorah's hill.

"That course—nor Delhi's kingly gates,
  Nor wild Malwah detain,
For sweet the bliss us both awaits
  By yonder Western main.

"Thy towers, Bombay, gleam bright, they say,
  Across the dark blue sea;
But ne'er were hearts so light and gay
  As then shall meet in thee!"

After a tedious voyage, during which the tracking of his pinnace by the tow-line appears to have been the chief means of progress, he arrived on 10th August 1824 at Boglipoor, where he rejoined, to his great joy, the Corries. He visited with considerable interest the monument to

Mr. Cleveland, "the father and friend of the Puharries," and examined the schools and other institutions which he had set on foot for their benefit. On the 11th, he set off, in company with the Corries, for Monghyr, which he reached on the following day. On the 15th, being Sunday, morning and evening service was held in a private house (Dr. Tytler's, the Garrison Surgeon), and the Holy Communion administered. Before leaving Monghyr he was advised by all the old Indians of the place to buy a supply of arms for his servants, and, being assured that a show of resistance often saved both lives and property, he laid out a certain sum in the purchase of spears, fowling-pieces, and pistols, so that he made his cabin "look like a museum of Eastern weapons." On the 20th August 1824, he arrived at Patna and Bankipore, where we was the guest of Sir Charles and Lady D'Oyley. He was much struck with the great, bell-shaped *golah* which he compares to the tower of Babel. He might well do so, considering its empty boast at the bottom, that it was erected for the "perpetual prevention of famine in the province." His reflections upon it are very creditable to him as a kind-hearted philanthropist, but do not show much practical wisdom. The *golah,* as it is well known, is nothing but a huge *Folly,* never having been used for the purpose it was built for—and never likely to be.

On the 24th, he went, by carriage to Dinapore, the Archdeacon accompanying him in a *tonjon*—"a chair with a head like a gig carried by bearers." He found the church held in a barrack-room, and in every respect shabbily, shamefully and badly appointed. The strong representations which he made probably put matters in train for the erection of the spacious, though not particularly elegant, church, which now adorns the grand square of the station. On the 25th, he ft Dinapore and arrived the same day at Chuprah. On ie 26th and 27th he was at Buxar, and on the 28th at hazeepore, when he expresses his regret that the money hich was spent in a costly but useless monument to Lord ornwallis had not been spent upon the erection of a church ith a monument to Lord Cornwallis in its interior. The ›se fields, he says, whence comes the *guláb-pánée* for which hazeepore is so celebrated, occupy many hundred acres, ıd are described as at the proper season extremely beautiful. 'n the 31st August 1824, he left for Benares; the current, owever, proved so strong that he found himself unable to dvance, so, after spending three days in futile attempts to ;em it, he determined to proceed by *palkee-dák*, and rrived after a day's journey at the station late in the evenıg.

At Benares Bishop Heber held a confirmation, visited the lission schools, threaded the narrow streets of the city, dmired the pagodas, the holy temple named the Vishvayasa nd that of Unna Purna supposed to be the Anna Perenna f the Romans, climbed the minaret of the mosque of Auungzebe, and thoroughly inspected and examined all the nost remarkable religious and educational institutions of the Athens of India.

On the 10th September 1824, he set off by boat for Chunar where he held a confirmation. He was much struck vith the strength of the rock fort of Chunar, with the quaint 'oller-stones, called *mutwálás*, from their staggering course lown the slopes to overwhelm and impede the advance of ın enemy, and with the large slab of black marble, on which, 'or nine hours each day, according to Hindoo tradition, the Creator sits, so that Chunar Fort cannot be taken except between six and nine A. M., when the Deity is supposed to be absent at Benares. He describes Chunar Church as of pleasing dimensions, solid, and in good taste.

On 15th September 1824, he passed Mirzapore, with the size and apparent opulence of which he was much surprised. He quotes the following doggerel as lingering among the natives at Benares, in testimony of the Sultan-like and splendid character of Warren Hastings—

> "Hat'hee pur howdah, ghoré pur jeen
> Juldi bah'r jata Sahib Warren Hasteen."
>
> On elephant's howdah, or well-saddled steed,
> Lord Warren Hastings rides out with great speed."

About the 20th September he arrived at Allahabad, where he staid ten days, awaiting the arrival of tents from Cawnpore. He mentions as the only considerable buildings or ruins in the place, the fort, the Jumma Musjeed, and the Seraí, and garden of Sultan Khooshroo. From Allahabad, having to proceed onward by land, he had to lay out a sum, which rather astonished him, in the purchase of a horse for himself, five *tattoos ponies* for his servants, saddles, bridles, and all the parapheruália of a march. At length, having accomplished all his episcopal duties, arranged for the prospective supply of a C. M. S. Missionary in lieu of a Chaplain, whom the people of the station petitioned for, and having witnessed the grotesque festival of Rama and Seeta, he set off at 5 A. M., on 1st October 1824, *viâ* Futtehpore, for Cawnpore. The march was much impeded by the heavy rains, which rendered the road often "knee-deep—middle-deep—half a spear's depth in water." At last on 9th October 1824, he reached Cawnpore. Here he found no regular Christian Church, but service performed in a thatched bungalow nearly in the centre of the station, and in a riding house adjoining the Cavalry barracks.

On 18th October he left Cawnpore for Lucknow. Here he had an audience of the King, Ghazee-ood-deen-Hyder, to whom he presented a copy of the Bible in Arabic. and the Prayer-book in Hindustani bound in red velvet and wrapped in brocade. He visited, of course, all the principal buildings and objects of interest—the Dilkhoosha Palace, Constantia House, erected by the famous General Claude Martin, and now occupied by the Lucknow La Martinière School, Sáadut Ali's and his wife's Tombs, the Roûmi Durwaza, or gate of Constantinople, and the great Imambarah ("or Cathedral") founded by Asúph-ud-Dowlah and containing his remains. Of all these the Imambarah, with its group of attendant buildings, appears to have most impressed him, reminding him, he says, of Eton College and the Kremlin. The Church services seem to have been held in the Residency, where, he says, "Mr. Ricketts acts as chaplain every Sunday."

On 1st November 1824, leaving the Corries behind at Lucknow, he started alone for Bareilly by way of Shajehanpore and Fureedpore. Shortly after leaving Lucknow he was taken extremely ill, and was in much perplexity being several days march from his medical adviser. The application of leeches to his temples relieved him somewhat, but his malady, which he believed afterwards to have been aggravated influenza, returned, and for two days his servants gave him up as not likely to live. By God's mercy, however, as he says, the remedies which he took almost in utter ignorance, produced an effect. On 6th November 1824, he was able to proceed on his way, and, on the 14th November, he reached Bareilly. Here he performed service in Mr. Hawkin's, the Judge's, house, and administered baptisms and performed several marriages in the residence of Colonel Vanrennen.

On 18th November 1824, he set off for Almorah by way of Tandah and Rangurh. He crossed the *Terâi* without accident, and, on 27th November, after all the usual perils, discomforts, and charms of a laborious march through the Sewalik Range of the Himalayas, he reached Almorah, and on the 28th, he preached and administered the Sacrament to a very respectable congregation in Mr. Adams' house, being the first Protestant minister who had ever visited the place.

On 2nd December 1824, he set out with Sir Robert and Lady Colquhoun for Chilka, which, though a poor place usually, is a mart for the trade into Kumaon, and through that country into Thibet and Tartary. The peak of Nundidevi, then supposed to be the highest in the world, was in full view from time to time. On 11th December he reached Moradabad, where, on the following day, he held service in the Collector's Cutcherry. Here he had an opportunity of seeing the way in which ice is made all over Upper India. "A number of earthen pans are placed on a layer of dry straw, and filled with water. In the night even the small amount of frost which is felt here is sufficient to cover these with a thin coat of ice which is carefully collected and packed up," and then stored in ice pits.

On 13th December 1824, he left Moradabad for Meerut. On the morning of the 18th he was met by Mr. Fisher, the Chaplain, at a little distance from the town, and pitched his tents in Mr. Fisher's compound. On the 19th he consecrated the Church, which he describes as a striking building, capable of holding 3,000 people, and adorned by a handsome spire. At Meerut he was introduced to the Begum Sumroo of Sirdhánâ. He describes her as "a very little, queer-looking woman, with brilliant but wicked eyes, and the remains of beauty in her features, of considerable talent and readiness in conversation, but only speaking Hindustani." He heard sad reports of her cruelty in cutting off the ears and noses of her subjects, and immuring one of her dancing girls in a living tomb which she kept guard over till the culprit was ascertained to be dead. Yet she professed to be a Christian, had a Roman Catholic priest for her chaplain, built a handsome church and convent at Sirdháná," (and, as is well known, she left by will a large sum of money in trust to the Bishop and Archdeacon of Calcutta for religious and charitable uses). Having spent Christmas-day at Meerut, he left it, accompanied by Dr. Smith as his medical attendant, for Delhi, which he reached on the following day. He found it a far finer city than he had expected to see, and the first view of it, as he rode towards it on the other side of the Jumna, impressed him greatly. He remarks upon the barren plain of sand that he was passing, that the floods of the Jumna in this region being strongly impregnated with *natron*, do not induce fertility. His arrival happened to be attended with floods of rain, of which the country was greatly in want, so the natives at once dubbed him in a *mobarak* (lucky) Lord Padre Sahib.

On the 31st December 1824, he was presented to the Emperor. Upon his entering the imperial presence, a herald "called out in a sort of harsh chaunt—"Lo the ornament of the world! lo the asylum of the nations! King of kings! the Emperor Akbar Shah? Just, fortunate, victorious!" The morning being cold, the Emperor was wrapped up in shawls, and reminded him "of a Druid's head on a Welch half-penny." After the usual compliments on both sides, the Emperor tied a flimsy turban of brocade round his head, and he was dressed out in a pair of common-looking shawls.

His attendants were adorned in still queerer guise than himself, "having their hats wrapped with scarfs of flowered gauze and a strange garment of gauze tinsel and faded ribbons flung over their shoulders above their coats." He then again came forward and presented the Emperor with an Arabic Bible and Hindustani Common Prayer handsomely bound in blue velvet laced with gold and wrapped up in a piece of brocade. We have not space to dwell on all the civilities and presents exchanged on either side, but he calculates that he and his party gave the Emperor gifts to the value of about Rs. 800, and received back to the amount of about Rs. 300, so that the Emperor was a clear gainer by the day's transactions. The only gifts, however, at his own charge were the Bible and Prayer Book, the rest being supplied by Government. Having visited all the principal objects of interest, Humayon's Tomb, the Jama and Kalan Musjids, the Fort, Sufter Jung's Tomb, and the Kootub, and spent Sunday, January 2nd, in administering confirmation and the Holy Sacrament, and assisting at morning and evening service, he set off early on Monday, the 3rd January 1825, *viâ* Muttra for Agra.

On the 11th he was at Secundra where he stayed a while to see Akbar's Tomb, "the most splendid building in its way he had seen in India," and the next day he reached Agra, the gems of which, he says, are the Motee Musjid in the Fort and the Taj Mehal. On 17th January he started on his journey towards Bombay through the independent States of Western India.

On the 18th he reached Futtehpore Sikri, and thoroughly examined the interesting group of buildings, which are chiefly the work of the great Akbar, and whose ruins are so vast and prodigious. On the 27th January, on his road between Bhurtpore and Jeypore, he met Sir David Ochterlony, the Governor-General's Agent, who was travelling in state toward Bhurtpore. Of this remarkable man's history he gives the following short sketch :—"He is the son of an American gentleman who lost his estate and country by his loyalty during the war of the separation. Sir David himself came out as a cadet, without friends, to India, and literally fought his way to notice. The most brilliant parts of his career were his defence of Delhi against the Mahratta army, and the conquest of Kumaon from the Goorkhas. He is now considerably above 70, and has often been advised to return to England. But he has been absent from thence 54 years; he has there neither friend nor relation; he has been for many years habituated to Eastern habits and parade, and who can wonder that he clings to the only country in the world where he can feel himself at home?" Every one, of course, knows that this was the man in whose honor the Ochterlony Monument on the Calcutta *maidan* was raised after his death. On the 29th January he was taken by Colonel Roper to see the city and palace, and to be presented at the Durbar at Jeypore. The Ranee, to his great disappointment, was invisible, and all the court civilities which he seems to have found wearisome and stupid, were performed by the Nawab. On February 4th, he sighted, at a distance of 7 or 8 miles on the right, a part of the celebrated salt lake of Sambur. On 7th February 1825, he reached Ajmere; on the 8th, Nusseerabad, where he stayed a week; on the 25th, having been travelling for some distance through the Bheel country, he arrived at Neemuch, where, on 27th February, being Sunday, he read prayers and preached to a congregation of about 100 in the drawing-room of a house built by Sir David Ochterlony.

On the 28th February 1825, he set off *vid* Pertabghur, towards Baroda. He was much struck with the poverty of the Bheels, and the wretched barrenness of a great part of the country through which he passed. At one of the villages in the territories of the Rajah of Barreah, he says "the headman of the village said he was a Kholee, the name of a degenerate race of Rajpoots in Guzerat, who, from the low occupations in which they are generally employed, have (under the corrupt name of Coolie) given a name, probably through the medium of the Portuguese, to bearers of burdens all over India."

On the 19th March 1825, he entered into Baroda. On Sunday, the 20th, he consecrated the Church, which he says is "a small, but convenient Gothic building, accommodating about 400 persons, and raised at an expense of not more than 12,000 Bombay, or 10,000 Sicca, Rupees! He paid a state visit to the Guicwar, which was returned with all due punctuality.

On 25th March he left Baroda for Surat, accompanied by Dr. Barnes, the Archdeacon of Bombay; he reached the town and cantonment of Kairah on 26th March, where he spent nine days, Good Friday and Easter-day being of the number. On the Sunday before Easter, March 27th, 1825, he consecrated the Church at Kairah, "a large and solid, but clumsy, building lately finished. On Easter Sunday the 14th April, he left Kairah, where his servants suffered much from the brackish and unwholesome water. On 10th April he reached Broach, a large, ruinous city on the banks of the Nerbudda; and on the 13th he arrived at Surat, "or, as the natives pronounce it, Soorut, a very large and ugly city with narrow winding streets and high houses of timber-frames filled up with bricks, the upper-storeys projecting over each other on the River Taptee." Here he found a very neat and convenient Church, which he consecrated on Sunday April 17th, as well as an extensive and picturesque burial ground "full of large but ruinous tombs of the servants of the Company, most of which are from 120 to 130 years old, and in the Mussulman style of architecture, with large apartments surmounted by vaults, and containing two or three tombs exactly like those of Mahommedans, except that the bodies lie east and west instead of north and south." On the 17th April 1825, he left Surat in a large lateen-sailed boat with twelve rowers, and at the mouth of the Taptee embarked on the *Vigilant*, a Company's ketch, which was waiting there to receive him. At sunset, on Wednesday, 19th May, the Bombay light-house was sighted, and at midnight on the same date the ketch anchored in the mouth of the Bombay harbour.

At Bombay Bishop Heber was rejoined by his wife and elder little girl, who arrived there exactly a week after he had done, having had a tedious and distressing voyage both from weather and sickness. On the 28th, he held his Visitation, which was attended by Archdeacon Barnes, six Chaplains, and one Missionary. On the 5th of May, the foundation of a Free School, on a similar principle to that in Calcutta, was laid. On the 8th, he went to see Elephanta. The stone elephant, he says, from which the usual Portuguese name of the island derives its name, stands in a field about a quarter of a mile to the right of the usual landing place. It is three times as big as life, rudely sculptured, and very much dilapidated by the weather. He gives it as his opinion that the principal cave was intended for a temple to Siva, the most popular deity of the modern Hindoos, who is sometimes represented in a triple form; and inclines to think that the sculptured figures are by no means so ancient as many have supposed, but have had an air of antiquity thrown over them by the perishable nature of the limestone rock out of which they are hewn.

Another excursion was to the city of Bassein "once a cele-"brated colony of the Portuguese, taken from them by the "Mahrattas, and lost by them to the English," and to the island of Salsette. The principal objects of interest in the island are the Cave Temples of Kennery. The largest and most remarkable of these, he says, is "a Buddhist temple of "great beauty and majesty, which even in its present state "would make a very stately and convenient place of Chris-"tian worship." Of the three residences which are appropriated to the Governor of Bombay, (1) that in the Fort, (2) that at Malabar Point, and (3) Parell, which is situated about six miles from Bombay, at a short distance from the centre of the island, he describes the first as a spacious, dismal-looking building like a German Stadthaus, and used chiefly for business purposes, such as Councils, Durbars, &c.; the second as a very pretty cottage in a lovely situation, and enjoying a fine view of the sea and harbour; the third as the principal residence, having a handsome interior, a fine staircase and two noble rooms, one over the other, the lower one said once to have been an old and desecrated church belonging to a Jesuit College which had fallen into the hands of a Parsee, and been purchased from him by Government some years ago. In praise of the Government of Bombay, and of Mr. Elphinstone the representative of it at that time, he says—after expressing regret that, if the English were expelled from India, they would leave behind so few relics of their religion, their power, or their civil and military magnificence—" yet on this side of India there is really "more zeal and liberality displayed in the improvement of the "country—the construction of roads and public buildings—"the conciliation of the natives and their education, than I "have seen in Bengal." Matters happily are considerably altered since these words of Heber's were written.

On 27th June 1825, he set off, with Archdeacon Barnes, on a journey into the Deccan. He crossed the harbour, ascended the Ghâts, and, having visited, on his way, the noble Buddhist cave at Karlee (which lies, by the way, very near to one of the stations on the Railway), reached Poonah, after suffering a good deal from sleeplessness and alternate fits of shivering and heat, on the morning of the 29th. Here he consecrated the Church, and preached to a large congregation, and administered confirmation to about forty persons. The church he speaks of as spacious and convenient, but in bad architectural taste. We have not room for his description of the cantonment and city of Poonah, of the Peishwa's palace, and of the large plain in the midst of which Poonah stands. On the whole, the place seems to have disappointed him, but he was suffering from sickness during the time he was there, and so may have been unable to get up the admiration which most people express in regard to it. On the 5th July 1825, he left Poonah with Archdeacon Barnes, rode down the Ghâts, the scenery of which he thought even more beautiful than when he ascended, and embarked at the little town of Panwallee, on the Panwallee River, on the morning of 7th July, for Bombay. He had a stormy voyage, got wet through and through, and the boat in which he was sailing filled so fast with the seas which broke over it, that two of the crew were continually engaged in baling. Having visited Tannah to consecrate "the small but extremely elegant and convenient" little church there, and having spent about a month "most disagreeably" in examining into the conduct and character of one of the Chaplains, he took his final leave of Bombay on the 15th August in the *Discovery*, commanded by Captain Brucks, of the Company's Marine. In leaving Bombay he puts down as the chiefest of all his regrets his parting from Mr. Elphinstone, whose unremitting kindness, splendid hospitality, and agreeable conversation he had enjoyed there—"the greatest pleasure of the kind which he had ever en-"joyed either in India or Europe."

Early in the morning of the 25th August 1825, the *Discovery* cast her anchor at Galle. The landing was effected under a salute from the Fort. All the principal inhabitants of the place were on the pier, with the regiments stationed there, and a band of spearmen and lascarines. The pier was covered with white cloth, and the Bishop passed between two files of soldiers to his palanquin, in which he was conveyed to the Collector's Cutcherry, where he became the guest of Mr. Sansoni, the Collector. There was at that time no resident Chaplain at Galle, but the Bishop found about thirty persons, chiefly natives, prepared for confirmation. The church, he says, was built by the Dutch, and, according to their custom, is without a communion-table, and for the most part open. At 3 A. M., on 29th August 1825, he was roused by beat of drum for a march to Colombo. The road was decorated all the way with long strips of palm-branches, and, wherever they stopped, the ground was spread with white cloth, and awnings were erected, beautifully decorated with flowers and fruits, and festooned with palm-branches. On the evening of the 30th he reached Colombo, where he was received by Sir Edward and Lady Barnes.

On 1st September 1825, he held his Visitation, which was attended by all the Colonial Chaplains and Church Missionaries in the island. The church, dedicated in the name of St. Thomas, is described by Mrs. Heber as a remarkably ugly, inconvenient building, not originally intended for a church by the Dutch. On 6th September, Bishop Heber went to Cotta, a Church Missionary Society's station, about six miles from Colombo. While he was there he received an address, giving an account of all the Mission stations in the island, and asking his advice on various important points, especially prayer meetings for mutual edification, and the baptism of native children. The Bishop replied to the questions generally at the time, and afterwards addressed to the Missionaries a long letter drawn up with his accustomed care, wisdom, and charity. The prayer-meetings he approved of, if accompanied with certain precautions as to the keeping up of the minister's proper position and apostolical character. In regard to baptism, the ruling principle he determined to be, that there should be a sufficient and safe guarantee that the child should be Christianly and virtuously brought up.

On the 12th September, the Bishop attended a meeting for establishing an S.P.G. Association (and it may be regarded as a general rule that, wherever Bishop Middleton had started an S. P. C. K. Association, Bishop Heber followed up the work by starting one for the S. P. G.). On the 12th he held a confirmation, and on the 14th he started for Kandy. The picturesqueness of the road is much remarked upon by Mrs. Heber. On nearing Kandy, Adam's Peak, about 8,000 feet above the sea, is visible. The Mussulmans have a tradition that Adam when driven out of Paradise alighted upon the peak, and a mark which resembles a human foot, is, they say, the impression made by him while expiating his crime by standing on one foot till his sins were forgiven. On the 15th, they arrived at Kandy. On the 18th the Bishop held a confirmation in the Hall of Audience, where the kings of Kandy held their courts—a long room with wooden pillars, having the lotus carved on their capitals.

The stay of his party at the ancient capital of Ceylon extended until the 19th, during which period they visited and carefully observed all the numerous objects of interest and beauty which its neighbourhood embraces. On the morning of that date they set off again for the coast, and, in a little more than a day and a half, rejoined their little girl, whom they had left behind during their excursion into the interior. Before their departure from Colombo, the Bishop received from the Colombo Clergy, with Archdeacon Glennie at their head, an affectionate address, which is written in such genuine and hearty terms that it is evidently something beyond the language of mere compliment.

On September 23rd he left Colombo, and on the 25th consecrated the church and, afterwards, the burial ground at Buddagame. On the 26th his party arrived at Galle, and, having been weather-bound for two days from the violence of the wind, they embarked early on the morning of the 29th, in company with "a son of Captain Driburgh's (the "Commandant at Galle), who was on his way to Bishop's "College as one of the students." On their arrival in Calcutta, Bishop Heber lost no time in endeavouring to make the best of his return to his centre of operations, and, having experienced considerable success in securing the co-operation of men like Elphinstone in Bombay, and Sir Edward Barnes in Ceylon, in the formation of Missionary Associations, he gave notice of his intention of preaching on Advent Sunday for the S. P. G., and of holding a meeting afterwards at his own house on behalf of the same Society; and at the same time he addressed to the Anglo-Indian community at large, a most stirring and carefully-worded circular, showing the folly and wickedness of being ashamed of our religion, or supposing that a bold profession of it as the means of salvation for Indians as well as Europeans, was likely to weaken the foundations of our dominion in the East.

On February 2nd, 1826, in company with Thomas Robinson Archdeacon of Madras, who acted as his Chaplain, Bishop Heber joined the ship *Bussorah Merchant,* and proceeded down the river, and, on 25th February 1826, they anchored in the Madras Roads. He was much pleased with all he saw in Madras. Having been requested to publish the sermons which he had preached during his stay there, he agreed to do so, and said he would take as his motto—

"*Crescite felices eoæ crescite palmæ*"

in allusion to the palm-planted compound of St. George's Cathedral. While there the *Caste* question, which had produced much disturbance in the Missions of Southern India, was referred to him. The Jesuits had humoured their converts very considerably, and so had brought over large hauls of thousands at a time, and some of the best of the Protestant Missionaries were inclined to tolerate *Caste*-feeling so far as to allow of some distinctions in seats at church, and in the order of coming up to the Lord's Table; but in the eyes of the more sharp and stern these things were regarded as a thorough abomination, the mere and simple introduction of a leaven of evil, which, if once tolerated, would gradually infect and kill the whole spirit of Christianity.

The question, therefore, was referred to the Bishop, and most carefully and conscientiously did he go into the subject; and the conclusion to which he came was, that *Caste*, in the converted state, ceased to be associated in men's minds with their religion, and was a mere matter of social convenience or hereditary pride, like what is seen in European countries. It was fortunate, in our opinion, for the ultimate fate of Christianity in India that Bishop Wilson entirely reversed Bishop Heber's decision, in which reversion Bishop Cotton expressed his entire concurrence.

Bishop Heber adopted much the same route to the South as that taken by Bishop Middleton, which we have already described. He found all the Missions, with the single exception, perhaps, of that at Tanjore, where an earnest and attentive congregation of 1,300 people made him exclaim "Gladly would I exchange years of common life for one such day as this," in a sadly decayed and dilapidated condition, and most earnestly did he labour, and with no little success, to re-invigorate and restore them. The hearty assistance which the Rajah of Tanjore had given to the Gospel cause, affected him so much that he composed a short prayer to be offered for him in all the Mission churches in the province.

On the 1st April 1826, he arrived at Trichinopoly, and on the next day, being Sunday, he preached to a crowded congregation at St. John's in the morning, and administered confirmation in the afternoon. The weather being intensely hot and oppressive, he was unable to attend the native service as he had intended doing in the evening. The next morning, however, he went to the Tamil service in the Mission church at the Fort, confirmed eleven young persons, and pronounced the blessing in Tamil. Subsequently he visited the schools, and addressed a number of Christians near Mr. Kohlhoff's house; he then returned to the house in which he was staying, and spent some time in talking to Archdeacon Robinson, who had been prevented by sickness from accompanying him, regarding the prospects of the Mission. The closing scene we give in the words of Archdeacon Robinson*:—

"He sat a few minutes absorbed in thought, before he went to the bath, which is in a separate building, a few yards from the house, and filled from a spring, considerably beyond his depth. He had used it on the two preceding mornings, and enjoyed it exceedingly. His servant, alarmed at his staying beyond his usual time and hearing no sound, opened the door, and saw the body, apparently lifeless, below the surface of the water. He ran immediately to my room, and gave the alarm with a bitter cry that his master was dead. On reaching the bath I plunged in, and assisted a bearer, who was already there, to lift the body from the water, and Mr. Doran and I carried it in our arms to the nearest room. Every possible means to restore life were instantly used, but in vain; the Garrison and superintending Surgeons who arrived almost immediately continued their attempts at resuscitation for a considerable time, but all hope was gone, and the blessed spirit was already before the throne of God."

Amid the tears and lamentations of the inhabitants of Trichinopoly, European and Native, the mortal remains were consigned to their last resting place, on the north side of the altar at St. John's Church, which is now marked by a brass in the form of two pastoral staves crossed diagonally and interlaced by a scroll, the whole being set in a slab of

* Robinson's "Last Days of Bishop Heber," page 183.

black marble. A mural tablet on the wall, just above, was erected by the Government of Madras, bearing the following inscription:—

Sacred
To the Memory of
REGINALD HEBER, D.D.,
Lord Bishop of Calcutta,
who was here
suddenly called to his Eternal Rest,
during his Visitation
of the Southern Provinces of his extensive Diocese,
on the 3rd of April MDCCCXXVI.
'BE YE ALSO READY.'

It is scarcely possible to overrate the service which Heber did for India. The exceeding amiability and gentleness of his character, combined with his high literary attainments, gave him an universal and almost unbounded influence, and wherever he went all good men of whatever creed or sect or colour at once rallied round him as a friend. His great research and unrivalled powers of lively and accurate description have rendered every place that he visited in India classic ground, and it may safely be said that most English people date their interest in this country, and their knowledge of anything like its present condition, from the period of their perusing his *Indian Journal.* But his greatest glory is, that he was, as Corrie says, so 'entirely a Missionary.' It requires a man of considerable powers of intellect, as well as breadth of view and largeness of heart, to wear the mitre of the Diocese of Calcutta with credit. Heber possessed all these characteristics, and so has left behind him a name which is, as Solomon says of a word spoken in season, "like apples of gold in a picture of silver."

LIVES

OF

THE BISHOPS OF CALCUTTA.

JAMES.

John Thomas James, the third Bishop of Calcutta, was born on 23rd January 1786, at Rugby, in Warwickshire. He received the rudiments of his education at Rugby school, of which his father, Dr. Thomas James, was head-master, and at the age of twelve, he was placed on the foundation at the Charter-house. In May 1804, he entered Christ Church, Oxford, as a commoner, where he obtained a studentship, and proceeded in due course to his B. A. Degree, after which he continued to reside as a private tutor.

During this period an accident occurred which is worthy of mention as illustrating his remarkable passion for drawing. A fire broke out one night in the college in the immediate vicinity of his rooms, and in a very short time his books, papers, and all his material belongings, were enveloped in the flames. As soon as the fire which at one time threatened to destroy the noble Hall of the College, had been got under somewhat, and it had become plain that the worst was over, Mr. James was struck with the aptitude of the scene for an effective picture, and, entirely regardless of the total loss of his property, selected a favorable spot, and immediately set to work, to make a sketch from which he afterwards finished a large drawing.

He took his M. A. Degree in 1810, and remained as one of the tutors of Christ Church till 1813, in which year he went abroad and visited Berlin, Stockholm, Petersburg, Moscow (at which place he arrived just after the burning of the city on account of the French invasion), Borodino, Smolensk, Kiev, Lemberg, Cracow and Vienna. On his return he published an account of his travels, supplemented afterwards, just upon his departure for India, by a series of drawings engraved on stone by his own hand. In 1816, he visited Italy, and, soon after his return, resigned his studentship at Christ Church on being presented by the Dean and Chapter to the small vicarage of Flitton in Bedfordshire. Here, in his leisure hours, he brought out his work on "Italian Schools of Painting;" subsequently in 1822, "The Flemish, Dutch, and German Schools," "The Semi-sceptic or the Common Sense of Religion considered"—upon which he appears to have spent considerable time and thought, and in which he refuted in detail, with much ability, the various arguments of the infidel—was published about this time.

In 1823, he married Marianne Jane, fourth daughter of Frederick Reeves, Esq., of East Sheen, Surrey, and formerly of Mangalore, in the Presidency of Bombay. The news of Heber's death arrived in England towards the end of the summer of 1826, and considerable delay seems to have occurred in filling up the see, for it was not till Whitsunday, June 3rd, 1827, that Bishop James was consecrated by the Archbishop of Canterbury, assisted by the Bishops of [Lo]ndon, Durham, and St. David's. He had previously taken leave of his parish, and, having now received the valedictions of the Church Societies, the S.P.G. and S.P.C.K., having been presented at Court, and having arranged to leave his two elder children with their grand parents, Mr. and Mrs. Reeves, he embarked at Portsmouth on the 14th July 1827, on board the ship *Mary Anne*, free-trader, Captain Boucart, and sailed for India on the following day.

The Bishop's party consisted of Mrs. James and her infant, a boy of five months old, her cousin, Miss Ommaney, and Mr. S. Hartopp Knapp, the Bishop's private Chaplain. They reached Funchal, Maderia, on 2nd August, and remained there for a few days. The Bishop was much struck with the fertility and beauty of the island, and with the liberality of the Roman Catholic priests, one of whom attended the service which he held. The line was crossed on September 3rd, Longitude 22° west, and on October 15th they reached Cape Town. Here the Bishop presided at a District S. P. C. K. Committee, preached to the English residents, administered confirmation to 500 persons in the Dutch Reformed Church, conducted a large and influential meeting with a view to raising subscriptions for building an English Church, to hold 1,000 persons, consecrating the piece of land allotted for it, and also another to be used as a burial ground, wrote a pastoral letter to the settlers on the island of Tristan d'Acuba, and endeavoured to compose a dispute between the Mahomedan Imaum and some of his followers, who went away saying that prayers should be offered in their mosque on the next Friday for his safe voyage to India.

The voyage from the Cape appears to have been very comfortless: the heat is often complained of as intense, and rain with closed hatches, close work, is frequently mentioned.

While they were beating up the Bay of Bengal, their supply of rice failed entirely, and their water supply had sunk so low, that they had it doled out to them day by day, in very short measure, in fact, the voyage continuing as it did no less than six months, must have been tedious in the extreme; but the Bishop's hopes were high, and nothing damped his ardour.

He laid down in writing, a plan embracing no less than five years for the inspection and visitation of every part of his enormous diocese, and occupied himself in working up thoroughly the scene of his intended labors, and learning the native language, in regard to which he writes on December 12th, "I now read the Persian character tolerably, and begin to see my way in Hindustani." At last on 16th January 1828, they reached the Saugor Roads, and the Bishop writes, "a little way from us on the left, or as we say on the starboard quarter, is Saugor Island, where a great fair is being held by the natives. Many thousands are there assembled, and we can plainly make out with our glasses the boats, and flags, and tents, and all the usual *paraphernalia* of assemblies of this nature. It is, I understand, a sort of religious festival, the main object being with each individual to stay a certain number of hours either in the sea or else in one of the jungles of the island, and, if they escape death from the sharks in the one, or the tigers in the other, they imagine that for this service their sins are forgiven them. Our pilot in running down to us the day before yesterday, fell in with a boat containing 30 of these deluded creatures, who had been driven out to sea in crossing the river to be present at the festival. They had been four days without food, and must have perished, but for his timely assistance."

On Friday, 17th January 1828, the long-wished-for steamer appeared, bringing Archdeacon Corrie, Dr. Mill, Principal of Bishop's College, Mr. Eales, Senior Chaplain, and Mr. Abbott, the Registrar, Mr. Cracroft, Mr. Augustus Prinsep, and some other private friends also had come to meet the Bishop. On the following day the landing was effected under a salute from the guns of Fort William, and he proceeded direct to Government House, where he was most kindly received by Lord Amherst. On the next day, Sunday, 19th January 1828, he was installed at the Cathedral (St. John's.)

As long as the cold weather lasted, he appears to have thoroughly enjoyed everything, and he applied himself at once to getting over the arrears of work which had accumulated during the long *interregnum* in the see, but as soon as ever the hot weather began, his health seems to have given way. On the 8th March he was only just sufficiently recovered from an attack, which had been subdued by large doses of calomel, to attend Lord Amherst from Government House to the ghat, at which place he took his leave to return to England. Having furnished the Bishop's Palace, (now a large boarding house) which is situated in Chowringhee, one of the southern suburbs of Calcutta, one and a half mile from the Cathedral (St. John's), "comfortably and handsomely" he began to take up the various plans which he had already formed for the good of Calcutta and its neighbourhood.

He got the town divided into three districts—St. James' District, comprising all that lies east of Simla Street, Hurry Ghose's Street, Wellington Street, Wellesley Street, and Wood Street; the Old Church District, comprising all north of Hare Street, Mangoe Lane and Emambaugh Lane; and the Cathedral District, comprising all south of the same. This plan received the sanction of the Governor-General in

Council, and was published with a plan annexed in a *Gazette Extraordinary* on April 3rd, 1828.

He also procured from the Government, after a continued and laborious correspondence, the right of issuing marriage licenses, and forthwith appointed the Chaplains of the Cathedral (St. John's) Surrogates, with a view to compensate them for the loss of fees which they had sustained through the division of the town into districts. He insisted upon an evening service on every Sunday throughout the three Presidencies, wherever the circumstances of the population rendered it possible, suggesting that it was far better to shorten the morning service somewhat than to make its length an excuse for only having one service in the day. He formed a plan for supplying the various Missionaries with books of practical information upon modern discoveries and useful arts.

He displayed a constant and kindly interest in the Eurasian or Indo-British population, and took every opportunity of visiting their schools, and presiding at their examinations. The Archdeaconry of Madras having become vacant, he appointed Mr. Robinson, the translator of the Pentateuch into Persian, to this vacant post. On the 27th March 1828, he consecrated the burial ground in Fort William, and afterwards the Church.

The following extract from a letter to his mother will give an idea of his diary:—"We rise at 5 in the morning, ride our white horses till a little after sunrise, return and bathe, breakfast at 8, then shut ourselves up during the heat of the day, unless any very urgent business obliges me to go out in the carriage, which I have aready been sufficiently warned to avoid as much as possible. The sun, our greatest enemy, is fully excluded from the house. Three long colonnades one over the other pretect the southern front; these are furnished with green blinds made of cane, besides which, the windows have also venetian blinds, and thus we exist without even a hint of sunshine. Such is the necessary caution for the preservation of health. As soon as the sun sets the European world is alive again. We take an airing in the carriage, and return to dinner at 7, and by 10 are in bed. . . . I have opened a chapel in the Palace, where the Litany is read every morning, and the whole service on Sundays for ourselves and our immediate nieghbours, for we are 1½ miles from the Cathedral, and must save ourselves the hot drive during the intense heat."

Again in another letter (to Thomas Caldecott, Esq., his uncle)—"It is a curious sort of life one leads here shut up for fear of the sun during the whole day; and whenever one steps out, attended by silver-maces (such is the necessary *etiquette*) and surrounded by almost papal honours. The Judges seem to live comfortably enough: they are not called on, except the Chief Justice, to keep up the state there that I am who am placed alone at the head of a department."

Having held a confirmation for 400 young persons at the Catheral, and having been to cofirm, and visit the schools at Dum-Dum, the Bishop was again taken ill at Ishera, the seat of Mr. Charles Prinsep, and remained for some weeks unwell. At the commencement of May, however, he appears to have recovered his health and spirits, and was able to visit Mrs. Wilson's school in the Cossipore road.

About this time he instituted an examination into the general strength and state of the various church shools in and about Calcutta, and found that upon the whole, taking the schools of the S.P.C.K., C.M.S., the Free School, the

Orphan Grammar School for boys and girls, altogether they contained 3,300 children, besides Mrs. Wilson's five schools, and the schools which were kept up by Dissenters.

On Ascension Day, May 15th, he consecrated the chapel and cemetery at Bishop's College. He had previously spent some time in regulating the affairs and economy of the College in which he always took the liveliest interest, and it was by his advice that the present dress of the students—a cassock and college cap—was adopted. He also obtained the consent of various Oriental scholars to be associated as honorary members of the College Syndicate, and formed a plan for adding a second court to the College to the west, similar to the original one. Among the benevolent plans which occupied him at this period, was a Sanitarium for Missionaries in the Nilgherries and at Koteghur, but he never lived to carry it out. On Sunday, May 18th, he held his first and only Ordination at the Cathedral, and, the following Sunday being Whitsunday, again preached there, though in such a weak state at the time, that he was obliged to deliver his sermon in a kneeling posture.

On Friday, 6th June, he married his wife's cousin, Miss Ommaney to Mr. Augustus Prinsep. The Acting Governor-General, Mr. W. B. Baley, gave the bride away. On June 18th, he presided at a meeting of the British and Foreign Bible Society, and became patron to the Calcutta Auxiliary Branch. In his speech on that occasion he mentions it as a well-known fact that, amidst the deluge of Mahometan superstition which has swept over so many fair portions of the Asiatic Continent, and overturned so many Christian churches that had been reared by the primitive labourers of the Gospel, a successful stand has ever been made by the inhabitants of those countries, who had once been put in possession of the Holy Scriptures in their native tongue,—the Armenian Church, the Syrian, the Coptic, the Abyssinian, and our own venerable Church of Travancore, at the present day bear witness to this striking fact. The plan which the Bishop had sketched out for his visitation of his diocese, enabled him to go through the whole of it in five years. Before embarking upon it, he instituted a careful examination into the state and condition of every station so far as the documents he had in hand could serve him.

He found that in the Presidency of Bengal, with its 31 stations and 29 licensed ministers there were only 7 churches built, and 3 more building. While in the Archdeaconry of Madras the destitution was almost as great, there being only six churches, and one in progress, besides the three churches of Madras and the two at Masulipatam. Especial mention is made at this particular period of a subject which seems often to have distressed the Bishop, and aggravated his ill-health—dissensions among the chaplains subject to him—but we are not told the nature of these dissensions, nor their locality. Probably the division of Calcutta into parochial districts, and the arrangement of fees, which that excellent measure brought about, may have been at the bottom of some of the mischief.

On Friday, 20th June, the Bishop delivered his first and last Charge to the clergy. The rains having not yet set in, the day was intensely hot. The Bishop was perfectly exhausted, and from this day dates the commencement of his final illness. Dr. Nicholson was called in, and advised him to hasten his departure up the river; and so, on the 24th June 1828, the Bishop and Mrs. James in one pinnace. Mr. Knapp and Dr. Spens in a second, and Mr. and Mrs. Augustus Prinsep in a third, attended by a fleet of carriage boats, cook boats, dhoby's boats, &c., 14 in all, set off up the Hooghly, having stayed a few hours at Chinsura, where nothing could be done on account of there being no resident chaplain at the time.

The Bishop arrived, on the 10th July, at Berhampore, where he confirmed several young persons in Mr. Smelt's drawing-room, as there was (and still is) no church at Berhampore. He was carried back to the river in a *tonjon*, or sedan chair. Before leaving Mr. Smelt's house he had written to congratulate Lord William Bentinck, the new Governor-General, of whose arrival in Calcutta he had just had notice. On the 11th, they passed Moorshedabad, the old Mahometan capital of Bengal, from Jafier Khan's time, 1704, till the British conquest. On the 12th, they were at Jungeypore, where they visited some of the Company's silk-works. On the 16th July, they reached Bhagulpore, where the Bishop was with difficulty moved to the house of the Magistrate, Mr. Nesbit. Here he grew rapidly worse, leeches and calomel were tried without effect, upon the pain in his side. Dr. Spens, and Mr Innis, the surgeon of the place, both agreed that the Bishop should be got to sea without delay. So an instant return was resolved upon.

On the 23rd July, the acute pain having given way somewhat, the Bishop returned to his pinnace, and, leaving Mr. and Mrs. Prinsep to pursue their upward voyage to Patna by themselves, set off as rapidly as possible upon his return. The south-west monsoon, of course, was contrary, but by dint of hard rowing, and, abandoning the smaller craft to follow at leisure, they managed to reach Calcutta by 31st July. Dr. Nicholson at once came on board and directed that the Bishop should not come on shore, but proceed at once to sea. Having written, therefore, formally to the

President of the Board of Control to resign his Bishopric, having taken leave of his various friends, and given charge of the diocese to Archdeacon Corrie, the Bishop went down to Saugor, and took passage in the ship *Marquis Huntley* (Captain Fraser) which was on the wing of departure for China.

On the evening of Saturday, 9th August, the Bishop, who had suffered all the way down from distressing sinkings and faintings, reached the side of the *Marquis Huntley*. A cot was slung over the side, and the Bishop was hoisted, without accident, lightly and easily on board. The sea at first seemed to do him good: he was free from pain, and for some days hopes were entertained of his recovery; but soon the shivering fits returned attended by violent perspirations and distressing hiccups, and soon all the last symptoms of incurable hepatitis began to appear.

On Thursday, the 21st, Mrs. James, who nursed him most tenderly throughout, communicated to him the fact that his case was hopeless. He received the announcement with resignation and firm Christian faith. On the following morning he received the Holy Sacrament from the hands of Mr. Knapp. In the course of the day his strength rapidly failed, and in the evening at 9 P. M. he quietly expired.

It has been said of Bishop James that the Royal Academy would have been a more fitting field for him than an Indian See, and we may allow that, before his consecration, it was art that he had studied, and by art that he had earned his name, but there is every reason for supposing that if his health had stood the climate of India, he would have made an influential and successful Bishop. His sympathies were broad, and his heart affectionate and kind. His legal knowledge was respectable, and all his state-papers, which we have seen quoted, are well and clearly written. His mind was fertile with plans extending over many years, and the only thing requisite to make them succeed was health, and energy to pursue them to their end. We could never suppose him reaching the same high standard as his two predecessors, but we can well believe that, under his rule, the diocese would have made good progress, his gentle piety diffusing itself quietly abroad, and helping on to the production of such happy fruits as make the vineyard of the Lord "a praise upon the earth."

LIVES

OF

THE BISHOPS OF CALCUTTA.

TURNER.

[THE accounts of the life of Bishop Turner are so few that it is almost impossible to find anything about him, the following is, therefore, a reprint of a notice which appeared in the *Southern Cross* of August 3rd, 1867, and the *Christian Observer*, of September 1831.]

John Matthias Turuer, D. D., Oxon, was born in the year 1786, but neither his birthplace, nor parentage, has been ascertained by the writer of this brief notice of his life; and as no memoir of Bishop Turner appears to have been published, the only accounts now available are derived from a brief *Obitvary*, which was printed by Dr. Corrie, for distribution among a few of the late Bishop's friends in India, shortly after his death; the *Annual Register* for 1833; the *Christian Observer*; some notices collected in the *Missionary Register* for March and May 1832; and a few other sources. It has also been stated that a "Memoir" was published in Calcutta, but this seems a mistake, and is probably referable to Dr. Corrie's *Obituary*, alluded to above.

Nearly all these printed accounts give merely the chief events of the Bishop's career in India; and they barely allude to the previous incidents of his life, which can, therefore, be noticed here very cursorily.

Having been sent to complete his education at Christ Church College, Oxford, he there received kind notice and encouragement from Dr. Cyril Jackson, then Dean; but his future prospects were wholly owing to his own diligence, talents, and integrity, as his father died when he was young, leaving a family slenderly provided for.

He took his Bachelor's Degree at Christ Church on 24th October 1804, at the age of eighteen, which was then considered an unusually early period, and his name appears in the class list of Easter Term in that year as *Maxima*, having been greatly praised by the public examiners. Almost immediately afterwards Mr. Turner was selected to be private Tutor in the family of the Marquess of Donegal, where he continued for many years, accompanying His Lordship's two eldest sons to Eton. From the Eton school lists, it appears that the present Marquess, then Lord Belfast, and his brother, Lord Edward Chichester, now Dean of Raphoe, and heir-presumptive to the titles, entered the lower form there in the year 1808, and left in 1811. He was afterwards Tutor at Eton to the present Marquess of Londonderry, then Mr. Stewart, and was on terms of great confidence with that family; spending some time at Vienna with Lord Castlereagh, and having been deputed to convey to his brother, the third Marquess at Londondery, then Sir Charles Stewart, the melancholy intelligence of his sad death in August 1822.

He had proceeded to the Degree of M.A. at Christ Church on 3rd December 1807; and in 1823 was presented to the

Vicarage of St. Helen's, Abingdon, in Berkshire, in the Diocese of Oxford, from which living he removed in 1824 to the Rectory of Wilmslow, near Manchester, in the Diocese of Chester, to which latter preferment he was presented by the Earl of Liverpool. It may be here remarked that the present incumbents of both Abingdon and Wilmslow are his immediate successors there. On settling at Wilmslow, he married a daughter of Captain George Robertson, R. N., of Edinburgh, who died only a few months before his appointment to the See of Calcutta, without leaving any family: her elder sister was the wife of the late Archbishop Sumner, of Canterbury, then a Canon of Durham Cathedral, and afterwards for twenty years Bishop of Chester, till his elevation in 1848 to the Primacy of the English Church. Lord Ellenborough, then President of the Board of Control, nominated the Rector of Wilmslow to the vacant Bishopric of Calcutta, early in 1829. The University of Oxford created him D.D. by Diploma, on 26th March; his Letters Patent were dated 16th May; and on the following day, Sunday, 17th May 1829, he was consecrated fourth Bishop of Calcutta at Lambeth Palace, by the Archbishop of Canterbury, assisted by the Bishops of London, Rochester, and Chester, (the last named his brother-in-law). The new Bishop sailed from Portsmouth on 15th July in the same year, on board of the British frigate *Pallas* of 42 guns, commanded by Captain Adolphus Fitzclarence, R.N. (son of King William IV.), along with the Earl and Countess of Dalhousie and suite, making a party of eight. Lord Dalhousie was going to India as Commander-in-Chief. They remained for nearly a fortnight at the Cape of Good Hope, and, after a pleasant voyage of nearly five months, arrived at Calcutta in the beginning of December following.

Bishop Turner was formally installed in the Cathedral Church of St. John's, Calcutta, on Thursday, the 10th December 1829, and on the following Sunday he preached there for the first time; the impression left from his discourse being that he had come to India, with "a spirit of Christian conciliation." On the 15th of the same month, his Lordship licensed as his Domestic Chaplain the Rev. William Drayton Carter, but he was obliged to proceed to Europe in the following month owing to sudden and severe illness; and in consequence of this unexpected circumstance, Archdeacon Corrie was requested by the Bishop, as a personal kindness, to take up his residence at the Palace, which he accordingly did, together with Mrs. Corrie, on the 18th of February 1830.

On the 6th of January 1830, Bishop Turner held his first Episcopal Visitation at Calcutta, when Archdeacon Corrie preached a sermon, afterwards published at the request of the Bishop and Clergy of the Diocese. Almost immediately after his arrival the Bishop had become Patron of the Calcutta Bible Society, and President of the Church Missionary Society, and appears to have acted on several occasions with more decision and desire for conciliation than his predecessors. Such at least is the account given by Dr. Corrie in his *Letters*, and he appears to have possessed his entire confidence. During the month of January a confirmation was also held of 317 persons, which, considering that the last previous service of the kind had been held in June 1828, shows a rapid increase of population. In Lent the Bishop catechised in the Cathedral on Wednesday mornings, and preached there on Friday evenings. He also visited Burdwan, taking a lively interest in Missions. On Sunday evenings he also preached in Bishop's College Chapel to the few students and others, and entered much into the affairs of that institution.

One of the first things which struck the late Bishop on his arrival in India, was the indispensable necessity of taking steps to encourage a due observance of the Lord's Day among the Christian community. Having only recently quitted a part of the world where that observance is *enforced* by law, he thought it incumbent on him at least to *invite* the voluntary practice of it in Calcutta, and by that means prevail, if possible, on its Christian inhabitants generally to set an example, which the Government itself, yielding to the force of public opinion, might perhaps eventually be brought to imitate. He was aware that his predecessors, Bishop Middleton and Bishop Heber, the one officially and the other privately, had endeavoured to prevail on the Government to enforce such observance in the public departments, but without success; and he thought that an application from the Christian community at large, after agreeing to conform to it themselves, might be more effectual. With this view he circulated a paper, inviting all sincere Christians to declare that they would personally in their families, and to the utmost limits of their influence, adopt and encourage others to adopt such measures as might tend to establish a decent and orderly observance of the Lord's Day; that, as far as depended on themselves, they would neither employ, nor allow others to employ on their behalf or in their service on that day, native workmen and artizans in the exercise of their ordinary calling; that they would give a preference to those Christian tradesmen who were willing to adopt this regulation, and to act upon it constantly and unreservedly in the management of their business, and that they would be ready, when it might be deemed expedient, to join in presenting an address to the Right Hon'ble the Governor-General in Council, praying that orders might be issued to suspend all labour on public works upon the Lord's Day, as well as all such business in the Government offices, as could, without embarrassment to the service, be dispensed with.

The expressions used in this paper, are those of the Act of the British Parliament which is in force on the subject. The declaration, as already stated, was framed only for Christians, and specially for those who are convinced of the duty of attending to Christian obligations. The purpose of the circular was to invite and to encourage the voluntary practice of those observances which in England are enforced by law. Christian individuals were invited to pursue a Christian object on Christian principles; and yet this measure, so strictly in accordance with what his situation as head of the Established Church in India rendered it proper in the Bishop to adopt, was met by a portion of the community professing themselves Christians, with a degree of hostility and misrepresentation, for which no difference of opinion as to the mere expediency of the course proposed to be pursued for effecting an object so desirable in a Christian point of view, can, we conceive, be considered by any reflecting person as a sufficient apology. When warned, which he previously was, of the obloquy which would probably be cast upon him for the attempt, he replied, "that personal considerations of that sort would never deter him from doing his duty." He persevered, and the result proved the anticipation to have been well founded. He had the satisfaction of knowing, that notwithstanding the hostility and misrepresentations in question, the object in view, namely, the due observance of the Lord's Day, was even here extensively promoted by the measure, and at one of the sister Presidencies his endeavours for the same purpose were afterwards still more successful.

As the measure above referred to was, we believe, the only one in which the lamented Prelate was concerned, that has ever been called in question, we deemed it right to dwell longer on the subject than would otherwise have been necessary, in order, now he is no more, that his motives and conduct throughout might be clearly understood and justly appreciated.

The next important step taken by the late Bishop, was the formation of the District Charitable Society. There was already in Calcutta a Charitable Fund for the relief of distressed Europeans and others, established in the year 1800, chiefly by the exertions of the late Rev. David Brown, which continued to be administered by the Select Vestry of St. John's Cathedral; but, however well adapted the Vestry may have been for the distribution of the Charitable Funds of Calcutta some years ago, the number of European paupers had multiplied to so great an extent, that it was become necessary to provide for the more full investigation of the cases of applicants for relief. Frauds the most gross were practised on the public with such facility, that impostors, speculating on the benevolence of the community and making, as it were, mendicity a trade, have, it is understood, found no difficulty in procuring from money-lenders, advances proportionate in amount to the probablity of success, which the acquisition of certain leading names to their applications for relief, justified a reasonable expectation of ultimately obtaining. To remedy these inconveniences, some comprehensive arrangement was obviously required, and at the Bishop's suggestion the Society alluded to was established. It consists of several subordinate Committees, corresponding in number with the Ecclesiastical Districts into which the town is divided, and of a Central Committee of superintendence. Of this Committee any individual subscribing 100 rupees per annum becomes a member: the former are charged with the distribution of the funds, the latter determine the principle on which the distribution is to be made, and dispose of cases specially referred to them for consideration.

It is necessary further to add only, that the Society has met with the most cordial support, both from the Government and the community, and its operations are progressively increasing, both in interest and importance. To the frauds above alluded to it has put an effectual check, by affording all to whom applications may be preferred for relief, the means of ascertaining, by reference to the Central Committee, or to the Committee of the District in which they reside, the character and circumstances of the applicants, and of procuring immediate relief for them if necessary. It is almost superfluous to add, that the operations of such a Society, so constituted and so supported, can be viewed in no other light than as a benefit to the community—a benefit for which it is originally indebted to the late Bishop, as appears from the following resolution proposed by the Hon'ble Sir Edward Ryan, at a meeting of the Central Committee, held on the 18th of July 1831, and carried unanimously:—

"That this Committee have received with feelings of the "deepest regret the distressing intelligence of the demise of "their highly respected President, the Right Reverend the "Lord Bishop of Calcutta, and in the painful record of this "melancholy event, desire to express their grateful sense of "those zealous and benevolent exertions which induced the "formation of the District Charitable Society, and of that "kind and unremitting atttention with which its operations "were ever regarded by His Lordship."

The providing additional accommodation for public worship, was the next object that engaged his attention, and arrangements were accordingly brought forward by him, through which no less than three churches have been added to the settlement. *First*, the church at the Free School, which will not only enable the whole of the children of that establishment to attend public worship on the school premises, but prove of great convenience to the whole of the neighbourhood in which it is situated; *next*, the Mariners' Church near the Strand, for affording the opportunity of Divine Service to seamen belonging to the ships in the river; and *lastly*, the church at Howrah, on the other side, which cannot fail to be of the most extensive convenience to the numerous inhabitants residing in that quarter. These arrangements were all effected without any expense to Government.

But it was not the spiritual interests of Christians alone that occupied his attention: he felt the deepest concern in the operations of the Missionary establishments generally, and in all proceedidgs set on foot for the purpose of disseminating Christianity among the natives, and for the furtherance of the views of the Calcutta Church Missionary Society, of which he was the patron, he was earnestly engaged in devising plans and making arrangements when his last illness overtook him. The Diocesan Committees of the Society for Promoting Christian Knowledge and of the Society for the Propagation of the Gospel, have recorded their greatful sense of the attention paid by him to the interests of these bodies, and at the Annual Meeting of the Calcutta

Auxiliary Church Missionary Society, held in the Old Church rooms on the 26th of July 1831, which was numerously attended, the following resolution was passed unanimously:—

"That this meeting receives with deep regret the sad and "mournful intelligence of the irreparable loss which the "Society has sustained by the demise of the Lord Bishop "of Calcutta, the zealous patron, and steady friend and ad-"vocate of the Missionary cause, and begs to record the "grateful sense which it entertains of the distinguished "services rendered by his Lordship, both in the plans sug-"gested, and the labours undertaken, to promote the inter-"ests of that cause, during the short period he was spared."

But the measures from which the greatest benefits may be expected to be derived, are those introduced by the Bishop to improve the system of public instruction, and which, had he been spared to see them carried into effect, would, in all probability, have realized for India as much as is attainable in this distant quarter. With him originated the *Infant School*, the first which was ever instituted at least in this part of India, and the whole expense of which was borne by him till his death. In the *Christian Intelligencer* for October 1830, this institution is spoken of as follows:—

"It is highly gratifying to see the facility with which "some of the children add and subtract by means of the "Abacas, and the progress the elder ones have made in read-"ing, writing, and needle-work, is quite surprising. Indeed, "altogether the scene is highly interesting. Every humane "heart must rejoice to see so many infants snatched like "'brands from the fire,' and placed in an institution where "their innocent and tender minds will be trained up in the "fear of the Lord, and in habits of order, cleanliness, and "usefulness. The Bishop of the Diocese has, we think, done "much for the rising generation in establishing this interest-"ing institution, and we trust the example will be followed "not only in all the parochial districts of Calcutta, but "likewise in other large towns, and also in the other Presi-"dencies of India." The plan of the *High School* was likewise arranged by him; he drew up the proposal for establishing it by proprietary shares, engaged for it the services of an able Rector, regulated the course of instruction to be pursued in it, and when opportunity offered, he gave it the benefit of his own personal superintendence. The nature of this institution, and the system of education pursued at it, were fully explained at a meeting held for the purpose on the 2nd of August 1831, at which the Honourable Sir C. E. Grey took a leading part, and at which the following resolution was carried unanimously:—"That this meeting receives "with deep regret the melancholy intimation of the decease "of their late respected Chairman, the Right Rev. the Lord "Bishop of the Diocese, whose zeal in promoting the cause "of education upon the only principles which can render it "beneficial to mankind; whose unwearied labours in for-"warding the best interests of all around him, and whose "amiable disposition, unassuming manners, and easiness of "access, must cause his decease to be considered as a heavy "calamity to the community at large, and to this institution "in particular, which has in his death to deplore the loss of "an able, experienced, and warm friend; and they take this "opportunity of recording their grateful sense of the services "he had rendered."

The graduated system of which he thus laid the foundation, and which was intended by means of the Infant School, the Free School, the High School, and Bishop's College, to provide for the intellectual wants of infancy, childhood, youth, and opening manhood, would have left nothing hardly in this respect for the Christian community to require, but his views, as already stated, were not confined merely to that community; he thought he saw in the state of things which had already been effected, an opening through which Christian instruction might be successfully imparted to the natives; and as he was convinced that no other description of education would ever render them what it is desirable they should become, namely, well principled, well informed, and well conducted members of society, he was, therefore, determined to avail himself of every favourable opportunity that offered for directing their views to this object. Before proceeding to Benares in June 1830, he visited the different native schools and colleges, in which so much progress has been made in the acquisition of European literature and science, and he was greatly surprised and delighted with what he saw. On his return from his primary visitation of the other Presidencies, several of the students waited upon him, and testified the strongest disposition to cultivate the most cordial communication with him. He had purchased, at a considerable expense, various astronomical and mathematical instruments, for the purpose of assisting them in the prosecution of their studies in the higher branches of those sciences, and he was in hopes that the minds of the native youth, who might thus by degrees collect themselves around him, would, in the progress of these pursuits, be led "to look through nature, up to nature's God."

But these hopes he was never permitted to realize, and all that remains to be said is little more than a recital of what took place at the closing hours of his life, and which, by those who reflect that their own last hour must sooner or later likewise arrive, cannot fail to be studied with advantage. It is not our intention to dwell on anything that took place during his visitation at the other Presidencies. Suffice it to say that he quitted Calcutta for Madras on the 28th September 1830, from Madras he proceeded overland to Bombay, from Bombay to Ceylon, whence, after having been engaged in various arduous duties at the several stations he visited, and having been exposed during this tedious journey by land and sea to the most exhausting heat and fatigue, he returned to Calcutta on the 4th May 1831, a dying man.* One circumstance, however, we cannot omit to notice, because it affects a body of men to whom the testimony of such an individual cannot be indifferent, and which, but for this opportunity, whould perhaps have been lost for ever. In a letter to a friend, dated, Colombo, March the 17th, 1831, he wrote as follows:—"I have been much interested by what "I have seen and heard in Ceylon.—A very useful lesson "may be learned here, especially important to those, like "myself, who are apt to growl at the Company's domination. "Every measure we would desire to see adopted in India "may be found in actual operation in Ceylon: there is no "restraint on colonization; the Government avoids interfer-"ing in mercantile concerns (except as respects the sale of "cinnamon and pearls); trial by jury is fully established; "in a great part of the island, there is an extensive and "systematic provision for Government schools, and yet every-"thing languishes: there is no spirit of improvement; in-

* In a letter from the Rev. Thos. Carr, Acting Archdeacon of Bombay, is the following passage. Speaking of the Bishop, he says,—"I "think, when he left Bombay, he did not expect to live long. In a "letter which I received from him from Cannanore, he observes in re-"ference to his feelings and expectations—'The way is rough, but it "is not long; we know in whom we have believed; we have not follow-"ed cunningly devised fables.'"

"dustry, either commercial or agricultural seems altogether "unknown; and the finest island in the world, rich in spon- "taneous productions, richer still in those which might be "procured by labour, with noble harbours and a situation "that commands the commerce of the Eastern world, is "scantily peopled, and of that scanty population a very "large proportion are miserably fed, and they are liable al- "most periodically to severe famine. What can be the "secret of all this? However, as matters stand, if you wish "to ascertain how completely good institutions may be "nullified, you may come to Ceylon, and on the other hand, "to know how theoretical evils may be cured, you must "make such a journey as I have done, through the three "Presidencies of India. I am satisfied that there is no "Government in the world so well served as that of the "East India Company; I mean that no service I ever "knew or heard of comprises so large a proportion of indivi- "duals able and willing to discharge their duty."

His health for many years had been far from good; he had long been subject to internal disease, but during his residence in Bengal his health had rather improved than otherwise. On his journey, however, a change took place, and after his return, the progress of decay became most rapid and alarming. As soon as it was discovered to be of a fatal tendency, a voyage to Penang, and eventually to New South Wales, was determined on, in the hope that his valuable life might yet be prolonged, but "He in whose hands our life is," was pleased in one short week to bring all such expectations to an end. On Wednesday, June 29th, a manifest change for the worse came on. He became sensible of his decay, but was not entirely confined to his room more than two days. Of him it may justly be said, "Mark the perfect man and behold the upright, for the end of that man is peace." As the hand of death became heavy upon him, no change of manner, no perturbation of mind, or alteration even of voice, except a little more of solemnity, was observable. He was attended with the utmost assiduity and kindness by his medical friends, and the Archdeacon had, from the departure of his Domestic Chaplain, resided in the house: with him the dying Prelate communicated freely on the subjects which occupied his mind. They were altogether such as might be expected from his previous character. The state and prospects of religion in India, the circumstances of some of his clergy, his own views of Divine Truth in the prospect of eternity, and the strong support they now afforded him; with such thoughts and occasional religious exercises, he met the last enemy, as one who had long been expecting his attack, and without the smallest sign of reluctance, yielded himself to the sentence incurred by man's original transgression. We have been allowed the perusal of a sermon preached in the Cathedral by the Archdeacon, on the Sunday after the Bishop's death, from which we copy the following extract of the character of this invaluable person, and with which this imperfect sketch may be brought to a close:—"We have left us in the character of "our departed Bishop, an example of one, who sought glory, "honour, and immortality by patient continuance in well "doing. He began where the Scriptures teach us to begin, "with personal religion. He had low thoughts of himself; "he was seriously affected with a sense of his frailties and "unworthiness, and rested his hope of salvation only on the "mercy of God in Jesus Christ. He had attained in a re"markable degree a spirit of self-control, so that he was, to "a considerable extent, a copy of the great Shepherd and

"Bishop of our souls, whose word is 'learn of me for I am "meek and lowly.' He took revelation for his guide, and "whilst the Triune God of the Bible was the object of his "adoration, the will of God was the rule of his practice. 'I "have a growing evidence,' said he, after partaking of the "Lord's Supper on the 3rd of July, 'that I know in whom "I have trusted, and he went on to contrast the uncertain-"ties attending the pursuit of science, with the increasing "confidence which the Christian feels in Divine Truth, as he "advances in the knowledge of it.

"In his peculiar office he came near to the apostolical "standard in the Epistles of Timothy and Titus. Of his "learning, and capacity for perpetuating an order of minis-"ters in the Church, it would require one of a similar mea-"sure of learning and piety to speak, but all could judge, "that as a Bishop he was blameless and free from reproach, "moderate in all his habits and pursuits, disinterested in "a high degree, and free from all suspicion of the love of "money; that he was apt to teach, and a true labourer in "the word and doctrine, sober in judgment, wise to solve "difficulties, of a compassionate spirit, and heartily desirous "of men's eternal good. In the public exercise of his "office, he must unavoidably, whilst human nature is what "it is, have given offence to some. The lively sense he had "of his own responsibility, rendered him more keenly alive "to such defects in any of those under his authority, as "might hinder their usefulness, or do injury to the cause "they had solemnly pledged themselves to serve. He felt "himself, therefore, bound, when occasion arose, to 'reprove "and to rebuke with all authority.'

"To the patient continuer in well doing a sense of God's "forgiving mercy takes even in this life the sting from "death, and an assured hope of eternal life gilds and illu- "mines the dark passage of the valley of the shadow of "Death. This our departed Prelate experienced: the per- "suation that God would carry on His own work on the "earth, and that He could and would abundantly supply "the means of so doing, left him without a care for this "world, an *assured hope*, that on being released from the "body, he should be with Christ, strengthened him to "endure protracted and intense bodily suffering, with "patience and fortitude not to be surpassed, till at length "being released from this strife of nature, he entered on "the eternal life to which he had long aspired."

To the above we will only add the last words the Bishop uttered, which, to those who had the privilege of hearing them, were most affecting, and which no one with the heart of a Christian, can, we are sure, reflect upon with indifference. After prayer had been engaged in, out of the Visitation of the Sick, ending with the Lord's Prayer, to which he added a fervent *Amen*, a short pause ensued, which was suddenly interrupted by his breaking out in the most solemn and impressive manner as follows:—

"Oh! Thou God of all grace, establish, strengthen, "settle us, have mercy upon all, that they may come to "the knowledge of the Truth and be saved: there is none "other name given among men by which they *can* be saved, "other foundation can no man lay,"—and he spake no more.

"I heard a voice from heaven saying unto me, write, "Blessed are the dead which die in the Lord from henceforth. "Yea, saith the spirit, that they may rest from their la- "bours; and their works do follow them."—Rev. xiv. 13.

LIVES

OF

THE BISHOPS OF CALCUTTA.

WILSON.

DANIEL WILSON was born in 1778. He was the son of Stephen Wilson, a Spitalfield's manufacturer, and his wife Ann Collett West. His mother appears to have been a most pious and exemplary woman, always displaying a deep and prayerful interest in the development of her son's spiritual character. The first indications of his ultimate career are found in his early years, when, he tells us, "he used to get "upon a chair, select a text and preach sermons to his "school-fellows." For a long time, however, it appeared as if both fortune and free-thinking were going to silence for ever these early aspirations; and up from the age of 10 to that of 18, when he was already fully installed in the office of his uncle, William Wilson, who was, like his father, a silk manufacturer, there seem to have been no indications whatever of the turn which his mind was destined eventually to take. Meanwhile, however, he was fortunate in meeting with an excellent school-master, a clergyman, by name Mr. Eyre, who had served for a short time as curate under the

Rev. Richard Cecil. Under him he learnt Greek, Latin, and French, and, what was still more to the purpose, he learnt to respect and love his dear master, as he calls Mr. Eyre; so much that he naturally fled to him for advice and comfort when the troubles of his awakening to his naturally lost estate, and his struggling to shake off the trammels of scepticism and sin came upon him.

At the age of 14, in 1792, he had entered the warehouse of his uncle, and perhaps, it is not surprising when we remember the history of that dismal age of Reason both at home and abroad, especially in France, where it had culminated in the entire national rejection of Christianity, amidst the horrors and excesses of the French Revolution, that the naturally acute and intrepid Daniel Wilson should have come out among the disputants—of whom it appears that his uncle's workshop was full—as an asserter of the irresponsibility of man for his actions, or that he should have behaved with marked irreverence during Divine Service, or that he should for a time have walked in the counsel of the ungodly, and stood in the way of sinners, and sat in the seat of the scornful! It was the way of the world, and especially of the young world, in his time, and he was never a man to do things by halves. His master, Mr. Eyre, had already said of him:—"There is no milk and water in that boy, he will either be very good or very bad," and happily an earnest word from one of his young companions under the preventing grace of God soon determined which it was to be. It appears that young Wilson had for some time been arguing that it was impossible for him to serve and love God, because he had not the feelings which were requisite to do so. Well, then, said the young man, "pray for the feelings." Young Wilson turned off these words with a joke at the time, but they made an impression upon him notwithstanding, and, lest he should seem not to have done all that he could, he did pray for the feelings, and soon began to grow extremely uncomfortable and uneasy about his state. It was a long time before he found peace.

Anxious letters to Mr. Eyre and to his mother and frequent interviews with Mr. Newton, of St. Mary's, Woolnoth, display the uneasiness and unrest of mind. He laments his levity, moroseness, overbearing demeanour, godlessness, evil thoughts, and intemperance in words, and fears he shall never see the goodness of God in the land of the living. Very frequently when he has broken some good resolution which he had made in the morning before he went to his business, he runs down into the dark cellar of his uncle's warehouse, and falls down upon his knees in prayers of penitence and self-accusation. Mr. Newton's influence upon him appears to have been of great value about this time, especially in checking his hastiness for results. "I don't like people," says that quaint old divine, "who jump into comfort all at once; better to go on gradually God says, the foundation in the heart and the walls no sooner peep above ground than we want the roof clapped on, but that wont do."

On another occasion he tells us he went to Mr. Newton, but found difficulty in expressing his wants, and so remained silent. On this the old man rallied him kindly as follows: "I can't tell what to say if you don't speak. A pump when dry can be restored by pouring in water above, so if you begin I can chatter for an hour, but otherwise I can sit a whole morning without speaking a word. Once set me going and you may get as much out of me as you please."

It may seem strange that while he was in such a state of gloom and uncertainty that he could have written such excellent advice as he did to a friend upon the subjects which he should choose for preaching! Begin with Christ, he says, go on with Christ, and end with Christ; and your hearers will never be tired, for His name is like ointment poured forth. But when his better self was thus minded, we are not surprised that plenary peace should in due time have been poured upon him in the reception of the dying memorials of a Saviour's love. He went to the Blessed Table of the Lord, and he was refreshed, and most singularly the earnest wish of soul so long in being eventually fulfilled was then strongest and uppermost. I have even wished, he says, if it were the Lord's will to go as a Missionary to heathen lands. It was many years, as we shall see, before this aspiration was allowed to take effect, but it is deeply interesting as showing the original bent of his mind when first he turned from vanity to serve the living God.

Immediately after his conversion the bent of Wilson's mind turned strongly towards the ministry, and great was his perplexity at the position in which he found himself. He was bound to an earthly occupation, which promised wealth and success, as far as this world went; and his repugnance to his abandoning it was at the outset most decided. Happily, he had a wise counsellor in his old tutor, Mr. Eyre, and by following his advice, and submitting for the time to his father's wishes, he without for an instant doubting but that the call which he felt was real, was enabled to wait patiently and prayerfully till everything came round, and the way was made plain before him. His father at last seeing that the thing was of the Lord, and that he could no longer gainsay it, consented to his leaving the business; and he was duly entered at St. Edmund's Hall, Oxford, where he soon became a diligent and successful student, and a valued and trusted friend of Mr. Crouch, the pious and god-fearing principal of his college. One sign, even at this time, of the high path which was in store for him, was the remarkable care with which the letters that he penned were preserved by his correspondents. They appear to have felt their depth, originality, and power, and to have laid them carefully by, and thus, long before he actually attained outward importance, he was secretly exercising it. Having at last obtained his degree, with great credit and the highest honor, he became a competitor in the university lists, and carried off the prize in the year 1803, for his essay upon Common-sense. It is very interesting to find that another successful competitor in the very same lists and in the very same year was Reginald Heber, and Wilson says that immediately after he had finished the delivery of his essay upon Common-sense, Heber, who had warmly applauded his precursor upon the rostrum, got up and recited his poem upon Palestine.

Being now fully qualified both in years and learning for his entrance upon the sacred ministry, Wilson sought for a true and thorough man of God to commence it under, and such a man he was not long in finding in Mr. Cecil who was already known, respected, and loved by him. Accordingly, he was soon installed as curate of Chobham, Surrey, and laboured there for three years successfully to form that peculiar style of pointed and telling address, for which he afterwards became so remarkable. He tells us that he admired his master so much that he had constantly to be on watch against copying him too closely and so making himself ridiculous. It is unnecessary to dwell on this part of his life. It presents nothing but the ordinary routine of a faithful and painstaking ministry, in which the body was broken under and brought into subjection, and the sluggish thoughts quickened and brought to light by a steady and persistent will, guided by the Holy Spirit. No difficulty or duty was flinched from or avoided, but firmly grappled with and mastered as it arose. It is a telling, though trivial fact, as to his contempt for outward appearances, that the patient helper of his parochial labours at Chobham, his horse, was sold upon his leaving the place to a neighbouring clergyman, with saddle, bridle and all, for the sum of 6 guineas (63 rupees.)

At just about this period that Wilson left Chobham, he married his first cousin Ann Wilson. These are his expressions upon the occasion, which deserve to be written in letters of gold:—"Oh God, greatest and best, smile upon our marriage; grant that we may love Thee more and more each day: grant that our lives and studies, plans and purposes, may all be in accordance with Thy will: grant that we may always look to Thee as our hope, our joy, our sure foundation, our all in all: grant that Christ may be glorified in us, both in life and death: grant that Thy Holy Spirit may dwell in our hearts as His habitation, His home, His ruling place, His Temple: grant that He may rule over us, sanctify us, destroy sin in us, make known to, and perfect in us Thy blessed will." They had in all six children, three boys and three girls. One of the sons succeeded his father as vicar of Islington. One of the daughters came out with him to India as wife of his domestic chaplain, Mr. Bateman. His letters and diaries shew how constantly he kept them all before the Lord in prayer; but he seems to have been too much devoted to ministerial work to enter much into their pursuits and pleasures. One son went sadly astray, but died penitent at the last.

The cause of Mr. Wilson's leaving Chobham was a call from his old college vice-principal, Dr. Crouch, to take up his place at St. Edmund's Hall. He remained at Oxford for 8½ years, from 1804 to 1812, playing the same kind of part there as Mr. Simeon did at that period in the sister university of Cambridge, as a fearless asserter of the truth as it is in Jesus. He had not however, like Mr. Simeon, a church and parish within the precincts of the university, but he officiated as curate of a small village called Weston, about 8 miles off. As principal of his college, he was honored and admired by the students whom he took every opportunity of cultivating and noticing, whose academical rights and interests he took care to advance and enforce on all occasions.

He was always a strict observer and requirer of academical dress, and story is told of his saying to one of his students that called upon him, "I am very glad to see you, Sir. But, Mr.——, where are your bands?" The same kind of punctiliousness as to decorum of dress followed him, we have been told, into India; and it is said on one occasion when one of his chaplains ventured to call on him in the hot weather in white trousers, that he said, "I am very glad to see you, Sir. But, Mr.——, where are your black trousers?" These, however, are but trivial matters. The influence that he had over his pupils was deep and lasting; they saw that he was in earnest in all he did, and they learnt to love him and admire him for his earnestness and in many cases to imitate him too.

Many anecdotes are told of the great power of his preaching at this period. Wherever he went he left his impress behind him, and the quickening effect of his words raised many a soul from death to life. Weston church was crowded from end to end, and whenever he preached in the university pulpit there was sure to be a full attendance.

People used to walk 12, 14 and even 18 miles every week to hear him preach. The divided species of interest, however, between his college and his church duties, does not appear to have been to his mind; it was distracting, and interfered, he found, with his spirituality and inward devotion. Hence, when his old friend, Mr. Cecil, again gave him a call to take up his place at the St. John's Church in Bedford Row, he consented, giving up a larger income in exchange for a smaller, but hoping by the change to secure the more complete devotion of himself to the work which he loved of—preaching and proclaiming Christ Jesus. There were some preliminary difficulties, and for a time a division of his labours between Oxford and London—which was even more embarrassing than Weston had been, but eventually he finally cast off from Oxford and embarked on the London charges.

It was no light matter to be the successor of such a man as Mr. Cecil, but by means of diligent preparation and hard study, combined with his fervency of piety and devotion, the large and distinguished congregations for which the chapel had become famous, were fully sustained and kept up; and all the while that this was going on, his pen was ever busy upon the prominent theological topics of the day, as well as upon the fundamental truths of the blessed Gospel, so that in every direction and manner the fertile streams of a well-stored mind and a loving heart were flowing abroad far and wide for the fertilization of the land. Meanwhile, many precious and edifying friendships were formed with such men as Mr. Scott, the commentator, Mr. Simeon, the Cambridge divine, Mr. Basil Wood, the minister of Bentinck Chapel, Marylebone, which were only terminated by death. The last-named of these gentlemen gives us an amusing account of Mr. Wilson's habits as a studious man. It was one of his sayings that "A man who was always to be seen was never worth seeing at all;" and when engaged upon any important topic, he was always most impatient of interruption. Mr. Basil Wood adds that many times when he had called upon him, under such circumstances, and in his own mind had scarcely yet settled in his chair, Mr. Wilson would start up in a hurried but very determined way, and say, "Well, my dear friend, you must excuse me; good morning, good morning, here is your hat, and here is your umbrella;" and before you had left the room he would be again buried in his books and papers.

Nothing was more remarkable in Mr. Wilson than the power and skill with which he succeeded on many occasions in solemnising without offending, in leading the company with whom he happened to be thrown insensibly and at once from the present world to the world to come. He never allowed anything like a trifling, profane, or ungodly spirit to pass by him unchecked or unnoticed, and often with the happiest effect he healed while he smote, and edified while he chastised. One instance of this is mentioned about this period of his life. On a certain occasion during a missionary excursion, a considerable company had been brought together at the festive board, where the provision was most costly and sumptuous, whose character was very little in accordance with that of the saint-like and unworldly. In due course the host of Mr. Wilson and the rest arose, and in rather an uproarious manner proposed the health of the deputation and Mr. Wilson, as soon as the noisy demonstration with which it was received had subsided, Mr. Wilson arose, and, after thanking the company very kindly for the hearty manner in which they had responded to the toast he went on to say, in those deep and impassioned tones for which he was so famous when much excited, that he hoped they would allow him to explain to them what, in his opinion, "good health" really meant, and then he proceeded to speak in such glowing and touching but beautiful language of the health of the soul, that every tongue was silent, and all ungodly joy and jesting vanished at once, and all present parted from him with the most sincere and heart-felt expressions of gratitude and regard for the useful lesson that he had taught them.

Mr. Wilson was incumbent of St. John's, Bedford Row, from the years 1809 to 1823. It is quite impossible to particularise all his labours during the period. They were manifold in every field, and whether he were organising the Missionary Association or the District Society, or the clerical meeting, or the Sunday school, or the parochial school, or preaching the funeral sermon of a departed friend, or advocating the cause of the sufferers after the Battle of Waterloo, or the British prisoners in France, or the various philanthropic and Gospel Societies, which he delighted to foster and take under his wing, he was always the same ardent, devoted and sincere Christian, with one end, aim, and object—the glorification of his Saviour—the edification of his fellow-men.

He was now 46 years of age, and serious illness for a time entirely interrupted his labours, and he was obliged to go abroad for his health. His constitution, in fact, though naturally most strong and robust, seemed as if it were about to give way under the hard work to which he had subjected it, and it was well nigh a year ere he fully regained his wonted freedom and energy. The return of his powers found him vicar of Islington, to which he had succeeded as a family living. One relic of his ill-health, however, remained with him. He established the habit of preaching in a sitting posture, and continued the same to the end of his course. We can scarcely but look upon this as an indication of some amount of decay of bodily strength, but it does not, at least for many years, appear to have at all interfered with the fervency of his appeals, and certainly for the present the mind was as clear as ever. Persons who have heard him, have described the great effect which he sometimes produced by rising suddenly in some impassioned and eloquent passage to his full height. They used to say of him on such occasions as they said of John Knox, that he looked as if he were going to flee out of the pulpit.

There were many bitters among the sweets of his parochial ministry at Islington. He had the misfortune to succeed a minister who was the very antipodes of himself in every way, and for some time his parishioners would not understand him. He had also a very turbulent and independent vestry to deal with—democratic and multitudinous, and very determined to speak its mind in a plain and sometimes unpleasant way He bore all, however, bravely, and in time triumphed over all opposition, and carried almost every point that he wished to carry. On one occasion, when an important subject had to be settled in his absence, he called his two curates, and, while the meeting was going on, engaged with them in prayer. In the morning, when the churchwarden called upon him to declare the result—which completely accorded with his wishes—he compared himself and his two curates to Moses, Aaron, and Hur, and said he felt sure that the victory would be on their side.

For some years now his thoughts had but turned to India, and words had been spoken by him at missionary meetings and elsewhere, which were very soon regarded, the course which events took, as almost prophetic. It ought to be mentioned, however, before we part with Islington as his scene of labour, that while there he founded the C.M.S. Parochial Association which now pours into the coffers of the Parent Society nearly one-fiftieth part of their whole supply. In the year 1829, his predecessor, Bishop Turner, had attended a missionary meeting at Islington just before sailing, and Mr. Wilson, who presided, had promised the Bishop that if at any time Islington could give or do any thing for the benefit of India they were ready. Little, perhaps, was thought of these words at the time, but afterwards they appeared full of meaning. When Bishop Turner died after nearly as brief a tenure of office as his predecessor Bishop James, there seems to have been a species of panic in regard to the Calcutta Bishopric at home, and no one could be found at first to take it. Mr. Wilson, however, had no fears. If none else would go he would, and so he nobly stepped forward to redeem his pledge, and happily, in the providence of God, also to redeem the See of Calcutta from the charge of deadliness and hoplessness that it had acquired. Little, indeed, looking at his three predecessors, Heber, James and Turner—the first of whom we saw, was his contemporary at Oxford—would it have been anticipated that Daniel Wilson's episcopate would endure for more than a quarter of a century, yet such proved to be the case. We must pass over the leave-taking, the episcopal consecration, and many other matters, and hasten on towards the rest. These words, however, deserve mentioning in connection with his third espousals to Christ, as he called his episcopal ordination, which are found entered is his diary: "Lord, I cast myself upon Thee, for discretion, support, guidance and help, I am a child, I cannot speak. Be Thou to me a mouth and wisdom."

There is nothing in the voyage to India which need especially detain us. The Bishop stayed at the Cape a few days, and there performed his first episcopal offices in confirmation and ordination. On the 4th November, 1832, he landed at Chandpal Ghat, and entered upon the administration of his diocese. The extent of the diocese at that time really quite takes away the breath to think of; where there are no less than 16 bishops now there was only one then—Madras, Bombay, Colombo, Sydney, Melbourne, Newcastle, Adelaide, Perth, Tasmania, New Zealand, Whaiafee (New Zealand), Wellington, Nelson, Christ Church, Brisbane, have all sprung up since Daniel Wilson landed in India in 1832. It was not, however, these distant regions that first or chiefly occupied him, although perplexing questions came in from them at times. He found multitudes of matters that required immediate settlement in Calcutta. The chaplains of St. John's shewed very little respect to his authority, and the vestry of St. John's appeared decidedly disinclined to submit the reins of their guidance into his hands. He had therefore, as he says, no position in his own cathedral. It was not till after much trouble that these and many similar points relating to episcopal discipline and economy were finally settled, but upon these it is not necessary to dwell. We shall endeavour, therefore, rather to select the most important point which Bishop Wilson settled, and the most remarkable works which he either initiated or carried out.

As soon as Bishop Wilson had got his proper position in his Cathedral established, he set to work with all his accustomed zeal and energy. He preached at all the various Churches in Calcutta and the neighbourhood in succession;

he visited Bishop's College, the C.M.S. Mission at Mirzapore, Mrs. Wilson's native schools, the Free School, and all the other religious and charitable institutions of the Presidency. He presided at the meetings of the S.P.C.K. and S.P.G; he became President of the C.M.S. Calcutta Corresponding Committee, and of the Calcutta Branch of the B. and F. Bible Society; he wrote letters to the ecclesiastical authorities in Madras, Bombay, Ceylon, Australia and China. Before the close of 1832, he married his daughter to his Chaplain, Mr. Bateman; Sir Charles Metcalfe gave the bride away. He furnished his palace, bought his carriages, arranged his domestic establishment, and, for health's sake, which like a wise man he considered of no small account, took 'the Hive,' a house at Tittaghur, for a 'Retreat.' He made the acquaintance of Dr. Carey, Dr. Duff and of the Governor General, Sir William Bentinck, with whom in their daily morning rides together he became very intimate, and of whom, in spite of their diametrically opposed views on many points, he became extremely fond;—extricated the Free School from a great state of embarrassment and difficulty into which it had fallen, and by inducing certain obvious parties to resign office, he started it upon a course which continued pretty evenly until the year 1865. He commenced his Lent Lectures, which he kept up with great regularity ever afterwards whenever he happened to be in Calcutta; he established rooms at Bishop's College which he called the Visitors' rooms, and to these he repaired at intervals to foster the progress of the College, and to keep an eye upon every part of its internal economy. He instituted a scheme for the introduction and development of a system of Infant Schools, first for Calcutta, and then for all India, and took immense pains to collect money to establish a great central

Pattern School at the Presidency, and to forward the movement in every way; a considerable number of children were collected, publicly examined, year by year before the rank and fashion of Calcutta, and everything seemed to promise the most abundant success; but by some means or other public interest in the matter first cooled, then vanished, and eventually the whole scheme proved a complete failure and was abandoned.

In his advocacy of the movement for a steam communication with India, however, he was far more successful, and although the natural progress of events must almost certainly have led to it in due time, he certainly deserves the praise of having led the van of correct and enlightened popular opinion in coming forward, on his own responsibility, to convene a public meeting for the reversal of a most inglorious and retrograde decision which had just been given by a former public meeting against it. In November 1833, the Begum Somroo's gift—to which we have already had occasion to allude in connexion with Bishop Heber—came into the Bishop's hands. Its arrival is chronicled by the biographer as follows:—"On November 15th, 1833, when the Bishop opened his letters he found one containing enclosures which seemed to give him the greatest joy. He waved two thin sheets of paper above his head, and challenged enquiry as to their signification. They proved to be bank bills, one for a lakh of rupees and the other for half-a-lakh, sent down by the Begum Somroo as a gift to the church and the poor. This truly royal gift was duly invested so as to yield an annual income of £380 to the Church, and £190 to the poor, and is now distributed by the Bishop and Archdeacon of Calcutta as Joint Trustees.

In the autumn of 1833, the bill for the establishment of the Bishoprics of Madras and Bombay having passed Parliament, Archdeacon Corrie was elected to the see of Madras, to which however he did not return as Bishop till 1835. In reference to the see of Bombay further delay took place, so that Archdeacon Carr was not summoned home for consecration till the year 1837. Early in the year 1834 the Church Building Society was started. The immediate engine of its origination was a letter to the Editor of the *Christian Intelligencer* from "Delta," who afterwards proved to be a Mr. Wale Byrn, a young East Indian of piety and impartiality, and chiefly upon the rules proposed by him it was founded, and has since been worked.

The following decisions of Bishop Wilson in reference to the vexed questions of Native Marriage and Divorce, which was much discussed about this period, are worthy of record. His plan was, where the law was yet uncertain, to decide each case on its own merits and gather a body of precedents which might help towards the formation of a righteous law in the end. A Christian man must be the husband of one wife only, and that wife the first married, whether she be heathen or Christian. If the heathen partner, as the Apostle says, decides to go, let her go; but let the Christian live without desiring a second wife during the life of the absent partner. No case, he thinks, can be found in the New Testament of two wives being allowed, unless the absent party have been duly separated and divorced by reason of unfaithfulness before a competent tribunal. He also decided that if a child betrothed in infancy became a Christian, and the party to whom she was betrothed was willing to give a legal bill of divorcement before they come together, she was at liberty to marry another man.

Having delivered his primary Charge on 13th August, 1834, on which occasion Dr. Mill, the Principal of Bishop's College, preached the Sermon, Bishop Wilson on 24th August set sail for the Straits on his visitation in the *Asia*, a large East Indiaman which had brought out Mr. Macaulay, the New Legislative Councillor and his sister (now Lady Trevelyan). He first visited Prince of Wales Island, or "Penang," (so called from the "Betel-nut" it bears) much admired its beauty and richness, took measures for restoring the dilapidated church, cautioned the Chaplain against the danger of being the manager of a nutmeg plantation which was attached to his house, and then proceeded in the steamer *Enterprise* (which had followed him from Calcutta), to Singapore. Here he took steps for the erection of a Church, examined the school, in which four languages—English, Tamil, Chinese and Malay, were taught, consecrated the cemetery, and then proceeded to Malacca, which he reached on 10th October 1834.

Here he visited the very ancient church, commenced by St. Francis Xavier, who visited Malacca about A.D. 1545, or dedicated tō him by the Portuguese in 1552. He called on Mrs. Gutzloff, the wife of the famous Chinese scholar and traveller, and was much amused at hearing of his recent escape from the infuriated Celestials in the interior, among whom he was passing for a Chinaman. He fell into the water and was in danger of being drowned, a Chinese woman siezed his long tail, in which he was figuring, to save him, and it came off to her horror in her hand. The cheat was perceived and he was obliged to fly for his life. Service was performed in the old Dutch Church, and then on the following day the Bishop set off for Moulmein. Here he went through the usual routine of a visitation, heard of Dr. Judson's labours among the Karens from an American schoolmaster who had been working under him, and sent the Doctor a kind message;—consecrated the wooden Church, which he says is "a beautiful structure just such as Augustine built in England at the conversion of the larger cities towards the end of the 6th century;" and on the 28th October 1834 set sail for Ceylon.

He reached Colombo on 7th November, and spent three weeks in his visitation, during which he went to Candy, Cotta, Baddygame, and Trincomalee. Various important questions came before him, among which the Oba-Wahansey controversy or the rival claims of the two Singalese translations of the Scriptures, one in court language and the other in the comman *patois* of the country, was the chief. The Bishop gave no decision in favour of either; but said that if both were circulated, time would soon settle which was best suited for the popular taste. Another was the question, what was to be done with the *Proponents*, a species of unauthorized ministry which the Dutch Government had raised up for the baptism and general superintendence of their *employées*, who were all obliged to be Christians. The Bishop settled that those who were worthy of ordination should be ordained, and the others should be drafted into secular employ.

The Bishop was detained at Trincomalee for sometime through rough weather, which rendered it unsafe to leave the harbour, but at last on 2nd December 1834 he managed to get a half assent from the Master Attendant to his departure. The steamer had no sooner started than she encountered a fearful storm, which continued for several days, and reduced her almost to a total wreck. She managed, however, on the 10th December 1834 to reach Madras, where the Bishop landed in the midst of a heavy surf which swept him and his whole party from the bench of the Masullah boat, and presented them at last thoroughly well dreuched and wetted upon the beach.

The great question which occupied Bishop Wilson during his stay in the Presidency of Madras was the Caste question, regarding which his decision, being quite the reverse of that of Bishop Heber, who was inclined to tolerate it with certain provisions, is very well known. In order to make himself thoroughly acquainted with the Christians whom it affected, and to give them every opportunity of pleading their cause in his own presence, as well as to make sure of dealing with them kindly and tenderly in a matter of such pressing and vital inportance, Bishop Wilson went down to Addalon, Tanjore and Trichinopoly, and spent many days in reasoning with the advocates of caste, hearing all they had to say, answering their arguments, endeavouring to convince them of its real and complete opposition to the most vital principles of the Gospel.

Hence he won many who had been opponents over to his side, and the general result is expressed by himself in the following words:—"A nucleus is now formed as I hope in all the stations for a sound and permanent Christian doctrine and discipline. One of the grand artifices of Satan is I trust discovered and laid bare. The new converts before they are baptized, and the catechumens before confirmation, will readily submit from the first to the undeviating rule now established." On the 2nd February 1835, he delivered his Missionary Charge at Tanjore and then retraced his steps to Madras, to which he gave ten days. On his voyage to Calcutta he touched at Vizagapatam, with the beauty of which he was much struck, and at Pooree near which he visited what he calls "the valley of death—the den of darkness" Juggernath. On 2nd March 1835, he was safely sheltered in the Palace at Calcutta.

Soon after Bishop Wilson's return to Calcutta, he had the pain of taking leave of Lord William Bentinck, who through failing health was obliged to return home. He administered the Holy Communion to the Governor-General and Lady Bentinck privately at Government House on March 17th, 1835, very soon after which they left for England. After this he was engaged in a controversy with certain of the Missionary body, Church and Dissenting, on account of the following sentence in his Charge at Tanjore:—"Perhaps not one in twenty of those who came out from Europe in all the Protestant Societies with the best promise, and who go on well for a time, persevere in the disinterestedness of the true Missionary." He steadily refused to retract the words, and we are inclined to think from their being taken offence at in so many quarters, that they were rather needed in the way of warning than otherwise.

After this ensued the settlement of a long pending question between himself and the Church Missionary Society in reference to his authority over their Missionaries. He simply contended for superintendence, control, jurisdiction in spiritual things over all persons licensed by him as Ordinary to perform spiritual functions in his diocese. And this, after a large amount of correspondence and patient waiting, he obtained, and got the principle generally acknowledged by the Home Committee by an addition of considerable importance to their body of Rules. In this respect we cannot but feel that most essential service was done to the Church Missionary Society in the matter of preserving its character as a Church Society, and preventing its drifting into the self-willed and insubordinate practices of Dissent. In the course of this year, 1835, chiefly through the decided measures of Sir Charles Metcalfe who had succeeded Lord W. Bentinck as Governor-General, he succeeded in getting his authority in his Cathedral, which the Select Vestry had practically ignored, legally and properly established.

But the great event of the year was the settlement of the constitution of the La Martinière. The result of the long and anxious debates upon this subject is very well known, and although the La Martinière catechism is not, we expect, duly dinned into every student of that institution as the perfection of Christian doctrine, it is notorious that all the salient and distinctive points of every Christian sect are carefully cut out of it, so that it may be repeated by Roman Catholic, Presbyterian and Anglican churchman *verbatim et ex animo* from end to end. It was by no means, however, Bishop Wilson's wish or intention that this emasculated form of Christianity should be all that could be taught in La Martinière. Originally he expected—and we ourselves thoroughly believe, looking at the terms of his will, that the Founder, General Martin, also contemplated—that the religious system of instruction in the school should be that of the Church of England. The Supreme Court, also, in drawing out its constitution had evidently, in the first instance, no other ideas, and had Mr. Macaulay's arrival in India only been delayed for a year, La Martinière to its great advantage, in our opinion would have been a Church of England School, but unfortunately Mr. Macaulay just arrived in time to upset all the plans which had been framed, and Sir Edward Ryan the Chief Justice was brought so decidedly round to Mr. Macaulay's view that there was no alternative for the Bishop, but either to renounce all connection with the

Institution, or accept a compromise. So he, and Dr. St. Leger, the R. C. Vicar Apostolic, and Dr. Charles, the Presbyterian Chaplain, set to work upon their L. M. Catechism, which the Pope, as soon as it came before him, pronounced an anathema and which we believe no Anglican or Presbyterian has ever studied since except as a literary curiosity.

On 13th October 1835, the Bishop resumed his Visitation, and sailed in the *Hattrass* pilot vessel for Quilon in Travancore, where he landed on 15th November 1835, and commenced his tour among the Syrian Churches. Upon this it is unnecessary to dwell. It was attended with attempts as futile as the previous ones of Middleton and Heber had been to raise the character and tone of Christianity both among priests and people. The *Metrán* was very kind and complaisant, though fidgetty and uneasy withal, under the paternal sort of lecturing which he got; the priests were obliging, and anxious to shew the Lord Padre Sahib the best side of themselves and their worship. The Bishop preached in their Churches, recommended the *Metrán* to take more care in the education of his ordinees, to live at peace with the C.M.S. Missionaries when they came in contact with him; and then, on 27th November 1835, sailed from Chetwa, opposite which the *Hattrass* was lying, for Bombay. He called *en route* at Goa where he was much interested in visiting Xavier's Mortuary Chapel; and Old Goa, in regard to which he says if "Calcutta is a city of Palaces, Old Goa is a city of Churches." Before re-embarking he went on to the large military station of Belgaum, where he preached on Sunday to a thousand troops, held a Confirmation, and gave the Holy Communion on the Monday, and on the evening of the same day set off to rejoin the *Hattrass* at Vingorla. In five days more he was at Bombay, where he became the guest of Sir Robert Grant, the Governor, and Lady Grant.

Having visited Elephanta, attended the wedding of the son of a rich Parsee, at which loose *wedding garments* were provided for each guest to wear, having had pointed out to him among the filthy Byragees—the man with whom Dr. Wolff had the following conversation:—Dr. Wolff, "Who are you? Byragee, "I am a god." Dr. Wolff, "You look much more like a devil:" The Bishop on 23rd December 1835 delivered his charge, and then set about preparing for his journey to the North. He bade *adieu* therefore to Bombay, and commenced the year 1836 by a rapid visit to the military stations of Kirkee and Poonah. Kirkee is famous as being the place where two thousand British soldiers discomfited a host of 50,000 Mahrattas. The course of the march to Simla is marked out by the following chief places—Ahmednuggur, Aurungabad, Mhow, Neemuch, Nusseerabad, Ajmere, Jeypore, Delhi, Meerut, Mussooree. At Ahmednuggur the breach made in the walls by Wellington's guns was still noticeable. The Bishop had great success here in inducing the troops to join in pledging themselves to temperance.

At Aurungabad, the city of Aurungzebe, the centre of so many noble and interesting ruins, the mausoleum of white marble erected by Aurunzebe to the memory of his favorite daughter stands conspicuous. In its tapering minarets, its faultless domes, its noble arches, its exquisite proportions, its rich surrounding foliage varied with running water, its ornamental interior,—it rivals the Taj Mahal at Agra. Amid all these beauties, however, of nature and art, there appears to have been a sad neglect on the part of the Christian residents of the duties and requirements of religion. The

Bishop's denunciations of idolatry in his sermon were objected to by some as *likely to offend the Nizam.* When the offertory sentences were read, no one in Church appeared to be in the least aware that they were expected at that part of the service to give alms of their goods ; and at the private house where the Bishop was entertained, when according to custom he commenced family prayers, the host would have continued quietly smoking his hookah throughout had not the Bishop, after finishing his reading exposition suggested that the noise of a *hubble-bubble* and the voice of prayer were scarcely in proper accord.

From Mhow, which brought the Bishop's party into Bengal, Archdeacon Carr who had accompanied him so far returned to Bombay. At this point a letter from Bishop Corrie was received, strongly dissuading the Bishop from endangering his life by a journey overland through an unsettled country, when the hot weather was just about to set in, and urging him to return *viâ* Bombay, but he committed himself to God and resolved to persevere. From Mhow he made an excursion to Indore the residence of the Holkar of the day (Holkar being a designation signifying that the seat upon the *musnud* appertained to one whose family was of Hol, a village in the Deccan), and held service with Holy Communion for the small group of residents there. Ajmere is described as a city clinging to the mountain side, supplied with sweet water from a noble tank or lake on the banks of which a hundred ghats, mosques, and country palaces produce a most superb effect.

The Bishop spent Good Friday and Easter-day at Meerut. Sickness was desolating the station, and he exerted himself so much in his endeavours to improve the occasion, in the way of warning, comfort and reproof, that he fell seriously ill himself and was obliged for some days to have perfect rest and quiet. He then proceeded on his way and reached Mussoorie on 16th April 1836. He found no Church at Mussoorie on his arrival, but before a month had passed he had got out plans, specifications, and an ample subscription list, a site fixed npon which he describes as "like Zion beautiful for situation," and on 16th May 1836 he laid its foundation stone. Immediately after this he left and travelled in his Jam-pan over a rough and somewhat dangerous road, in 18 days to Simla; which, amid storms of thunder and rain, with tents saturated, and all suffering in health except himself, he reached on 3rd June 1836.

He employed his leisure here in preparing for the press, a volume of "Sermons preached in India," arranged in a series calculated to shew the "Tendency of Christianity," and on 10th October quitted Simla to rejoin his camp which had been assembled at the foot of the hills. Travelling leisurely downwards and staying awhile *en route* to accustom himself to the change of climate, he struck in to the plains on the 17th. In two days he reached the Sutlej, the bounary of Alexander's Indian Expedition at Roopur, where Lord William Bentinck met Runjeet Singh, and there took ship and glided down the stream towards Loodianah. It was in the course of this voyage that he rose suddenly from his seat and, looking towards the Punjab, said aloud, "I take possession of this land in the name of my Lord and Master Jesus Christ." The propriety of this speech has been much commented upon. It has been sneered at as bombastic, indecent, presumptuous; but it is certainly singular that within a dozen years the Punjab should have passed under our rule at the cost of little blood and treasure, and that the prospects of the Missionary cause there should at the present time be singularly favourable.

At Loodianah he set matters in train for the erection of a Church which is now Christ Church, Loodianah. He also had an interesting interview with Shah Soojah, the ex-king of Cabul, and his brother Shah Zemaun who had had his eyes put out. He exhorted the former to contentment with his lot, but when pointedly asked if *he* would like to be turned out of *his* bishopric and cast adrift, was obliged to allow that he would not. "No more do I, said Shah Soojah, "like being turned out of my throne." Shah Soojah was afterwards restored to his throne by the British.

By way of Umballa, the Bishop passed on to Kurnaul, resting one night at Thanesir, famous for its magnificent temples, immense tanks, and very holy Brahmins. Here he had a very striking instance of the value of Dr. Mill's great work, the "Christa Sangita," a scheme of the Christian religion in Sanscrit verse : A Christian pundit read it aloud to the admiring Brahmins the whole night through, and still they kept asking for more ; coming at last to the conclusion that "no mere mortal man could have written such a book" and that the Bishop (who had been the means of their hearing it) must be an angel ! At Kurnal the Bishop ordained Annund Musseeh, the first native that he admitted to Holy Orders. On 18th November 1836 he reached Delhi. Here he consecrated the Church which Colonel Skinner had erected in fulfilment of a vow made 20 years before. In spite of his Mahometan wife, the Bishop regarded him with great favour, called the Church St. James', after him, and admitted him and his two sons as candidates for confirmation.

About the middle of December he entered Agra, where he found as Governor his old friend Sir Charles Metcalfe, who had officiated temporarily as Governor-General, with whom he stayed three weeks. By way of Allyghur, where he performed all duties and examined the wonderful Fort, he passed on to Bareilly. Here in spite of the stout opposition of the Brigadier he got up a subscription for a Church, which is now Christ Church, Bareilly. Futtehgurh, Cawnpore, and Lucknow at each of which he laid the foundation of two Churches, Allahabad, where he indited a strong personal remonstrance to the Governor-General against the Pilgrim-tax, and heard of the death of Bishop Corrie, Mirzapore, Chunar, Benares, Ghazepore, Buxar, Dinapore, Monghyr, Bhagulpore and Rampore Bauleah, were successively visited, and on 13th March 1837 the steamer was at Saugor. On the following morning Archdeacon Dealtry and Dr. Mill came on board. In the afternoon the Bishop went to pay his respects to the new Governor-General, Lord Auckland, and the Misses Eden, and at 4 o'clock he reached his Palace in health and safety.

His first duty after his arrival was to preach Bishop Corrie's funeral sermon, which he did at St. Johns' to a crowded congregation. The usual services of Passion Week and Easter followed, and the usual routine of episcopal duties at the Presidency. The season proved unusually hot. The Bishop sought relief by taking a country house 'Shalimar' across the river, and in July and August filled up a few gaps in the close of his tour by going to Chinsurah, Bancoorah, Burdwan and Krishnaghur. At Burdwan he was much struck with Mr. Weitbrecht's labours the "neat and appropriate" Church which he had built, his gardens, schools and native christian village. In the course of this summer the Bishop had the pain of parting from Dr. Mill and from his Domestic Chaplain Mr. Bateman, who both went home out of health. He also lost in October his friend Sir Benjamin Malkin, Judge of the Supreme Court, to whom he was much attached.

On 6th July 1838, Bishop Wilson commenced his second Visitation by delivering his Charge in Calcutta, the main feature of which was a strong protest against the principles of the Tractarians. On the 22nd July, he was off in the brig *Hattrass* for the Straits. He visited Penang, Malacca and Singapore. At the last named place, he found the church which he had planned ready, but a dispute had occurred in reference to its consecration in censequence of the Dissenters, who had subscribed to its erection, putting in a claim to it. However he managed to bring them round, and having received a petition, signed by 54 residents, consecrated the building using the expression that "he had never seen a whole community come round so well." He then proceeded to Chittagong, where he laid the foundation of a church, and visited with much interest a house called "Jaffierbad," enjoying a lovely sea view, which had been a favorite residence of Sir William Jones.

On 23rd November, he reached Calcutta. On the 9th January 1839, he was cheered by the arrival of his new Domestic Chaplain, the Rev. John Henry Pratt, whom he greeted with particular pleasure, not only because he was the son of an old friend, but also because he had had no regular domestic chaplain since the departure of his son-in-law Mr. Bateman, on 4th September 1837. Shortly after Mr. Pratt's arrival, Mr. Withers, the Principal of Bishop's College, being ordered to sea on account of ill-health, and Mr. Malan, through failing eyesight, being obliged to go to England, the Bishop, assisted by Mr. Pratt, undertook the professional duties of the College and carried them on for some time. In the Lent of 1839, the Lectures "on the Lord's Prayer" were delivered to crowded congregations at St. John's. At the last of these, "where nearly 1,200 of the *élite* of Calcutta were present," he announced his intention of building a new cathedral to be called St. Paul's and having made all arrangements with his usual promptitude for carrying on the work, on Tuesday, the 8th October 1839, he laid the foundation-stone.

About this time there was a wonderful awakening among the Christians at Krishnaghur. Village after village came forward pressing for baptism, and having sent Archdeacon Dealtry, the Revs. K. M. Bannerjee, Weitbrecht, and Saudys, to enquire into and report upon the movement, he himself afterwards went down to help on the good work. From the district of Krishnaghur, he proceeded on his Visitation north-westwards, passing through Berhampore, Bauleah, Patna, Gya, Hazareebaugh, Ghazeepore, Jounpore, Benares, Allahabad, Cawnpore, Lucknow, Bareilly, Delhi, Almorah, Mussoorie to Simla, where he was safely housed on 21st May 1840. Here he stayed till Monday the 26th October, occupying himself as usual in reading, writing, preaching, assisting in works of charity, and giving "dozens of little, quiet, cheerful dinner-parties;" and then returned by way of Subathoo, Loodianah, Kurnaul, Paniput, Delhi, Allyghur, Agra, Gwalior, Jhansi, Saugor, Jubbulpore, Allahabad, Goruckpore, Krishnaghur to Calcutta, which he reached on 3rd April 1841.

He found Mr. Street, the new Principal of Bishop's College arrived, of whom he very soon began to complain as imbued and steeped in Tractarianism. He wrote at length to the S. P. G. at home who, it seems, had had an idea of sending out Mr. Manning (the present R. C. Archbishop of

Westminster), but had declined doing so from his extreme views, entreating them to recall Mr. Street: but they did not exactly see their way to this.

On the 7th September, the Bishop writes in his journal letters, "We have formed our Additional Clergy Society resembling your 'Additional Curates' and Pastoral Aid' Societies. I cannot but think, if God blesses, it will be a glorious thing for the Diocese." The idea of this Society was first brought into practical shape about 10 months before in a conversation at Agra, during the Bishop's late tour with the Lieutenant Governor, N. W. P., Mr. Robertson, and Mr. Thomason; and in the course of that period the scheme had been matured and got into work.

Dacca, Sylhet, Cherrapoonjee, and Burrisaul were visited during the October and November of 1841. At Cherrapoonjee, the Bishop received the somewhat singular present of one thousand oranges from Mr. George Inglis, in whose memory the painted window which adorns the east end of St. John's Church was erected by his widow. Advent 1841 was spent in Calcutta. During this season came the terrible news of the Caubul tragedy. In March 1842, Lord Ellenborough arrived and Lord Auckland went home. Bishop Wilson commenced his first Metropolitical and third Diocesan Visitation, by delivering, at Calcutta, on 24th August 1842 his third Charge. Like the last, it was a bold and uncompromising denouncement of Tractarianism, and assertion of Holy Scripture as containing the sole Rule of Faith. He had some difficulty in persuading the Directors that a Metropolitan's visitation once in five years, thougth according to the letter of the Act of Parliament which authorized it, was necessary, but at last he got it allowed, and by the same despatch he received the news that his representations in reference to the increase of the staff of Chaplains had been attended to by raising the number to 51, with an allotment of 12 assistant Chaplains in anticipation of vacancies, whereby all delay in filling up the gaps in the ecclesiastical service might be avoided. He also obtained leave for himself and his Suffragans of Madras and Bombay for 18 months furlough, with allowances after 10 years' service.

On the evening of the day on which he delivered his charge, 24th August 1842, he embarked with Mr. Pratt, and Dr. Goodeve, for the Straits. Moulmein, Penang, Malacca, and Singapore were visited, and then he stretched across to Madras, where, in a constant and close intercourse with Bishop Spencer, Archdeacon Harper, and the Rev. J. Tucker, Secretary, Church Missionary Society, he spent 20 days. He then went on by sea, *viá* Negapatam, to Tanjore and Trichinopoly. He found the caste question still disturbing the churches, and once more raised his voice against it. We may venture here to say that probably the whole question would have been settled before now, and the battlers for such an outrageous anomaly as the acknowledgment of any thing but the equality of all men in the House of Almighty God would have been altogether beaten out of the field; but unfortunately some Lutheran missionaries, who admit caste distinctions, have harboured the seceders, so that the evil is not even yet stamped out.

Passing by way of Trivandrum, Quilon, Cottayam, through the Syrian churches, and having found that all his attempts at their improvement were utterly futile, he went on to Alleppee and Cochin and then to Bombay which he reached 13th March 1843. Here he delivered his Charge, enjoyed much pleasant converse with the Governor, Sir George Arthur, and Bishop Carr, whom he describes as "an angel," so sweet, humble, and spiritually minded; and then, on 3rd April, embarked for Calcutta, which, touching *en route* at Goa, he reached on 12th May 1843.

The progress of the new Cathedral is thus noted on July 10th: "We are now raising the walls of our Tower. We have funds for a year or more from this time. Then our way I expect will be dark and boggy. Vast supplies required, and everything standing still. A grand effort will be required to raise subscriptions."

There are indications in his correspondence during this summer that his health was failing. He had had an attack of the gout on his voyage from Bombay, and, on August 11th, he writes: "I have not been well. I have not the strength or spirits I had. I have not preached for sometime, and I doubt whether I shall ever be myself again." It was therefore a great relief to him on 17th October to leave Calcutta for a visitation of the Upper Provinces and a retreat to the Hills. He went up the river through the underbunds in a *Flat*, accompanied by Mr. Pratt, Captain Philpotts (son of the Bishop of Exeter), Dr. Bell and several other persons. At Ghazeepore, he left the river and passed through Goruckpore, Benares, Allahabad, Futtehpore, Futtehghur, Bareilly, Nynee Tal, Almorah, Meerut, and Mussoorie to Simla. Here he prepared for publication his Lent Lectures on the Epistle to the Colossians; helped to build a new church, and received some munificent gifts from Mr. Gordon, and others, for his Cathedral and for the Additional Clergy Society.

On 17th October 1844, he left Simla. Writing on the march downwards between Loodianah and Umballa, he says: "From the new Governor-General Lord Hardinge, I have a charming letter in answer to mine, placing 1,500 rupees at my disposal for charity, and promising me all aid." On the 17th November, at Umballah, he was taken seriously ill with fever, and the attack continued so long, and left him so completely prostrate, that with every possible precaution it was almost impossible to make any progress with the march; at last he reached Allyghur, and on 23rd January 1845, he wrote thence to his children, announcing his hope of seeing them *Deo favente* ere long at home. He arrived in Calcutta on 26th April, and at once met Colonel Forbes at the Cathedral, which had now received the gilded arrow, nine feet long in the summit of the spire. He called it "a pledge of the arrow of the Lord's deliverance for India, and of the Messiah's doctrine, being, like arrows, sharp in the heart of the king's enemies, so that the people may fall under it in penitence, faith, and allegiance."*

Before departing for England, he held his fourth Visitation. His Charge on this occasion being his fourth charge, was read to the clergy by the Archdeacon and Mr. Pratt, he being too feeble to read it himself. On the 3rd March 1845, he left in the *Precursor* steamer for England *viâ* the Red Sea.

It will be unnecessary for us to go into all the particulars of the visit to England. There were of course the usual greetings of friends, receptions, addresses, dinners, speeches, and so forth. When the S.P.G. Committee presented him with their congratulations, he took occasion to read them a good, sound, and carefully written lecture against Tractarianism. Wherever he went he did not forget his great work—the Cathedral; and copious subscriptions to it poured

* This arrow being of copper, was stolen by the workmen who were repairing the Cathedral in 1869 but has been replaced by one of iron-gilt.

in from every quarter. The Lord Mayor gave the use of the Guildhall for the exhibition of Messrs. Gray and Co's Organ, built for it. Tickeets were sold, and the sums realized went to the Cathedral Fund. He shewed the Queen, Prince Albert, and Sir Robert Peel, his cathedral plans, and the Queen gave the Communion Plate for it—"ten pieces of silver plate, richly gilded, and bearing suitable inscriptions." The Dean and Chapter of Windsor gave a large painted East Window by West.* On the whole, for various purposes connected with the Cathedral, upwards of a lakh and a half of rupees were realized. At last, having spent nearly 20 months in his native land, very much to his heart's content, and somewhat to the benefit of his health, he again set his face Eastward, and to avoid the fatigue of the overland journey, sailed in the *Prince of Wales*, 1350 tons, Captain Hopkins, *viâ* the Cape, for Calcutta; leaving Portsmouth on 31st August, and arriving in Calcutta on the 14th December 1846.

It was evident that although his health had benefited somewhat by his *magical* visit home—as he calls it—he was no longer equal to the incessant labour and hard toil which he had gone through in previous years. He himself felt that he must "go softly and take in sail," and constant entries occur in his letters in reference to the infirmities with which he was beset. He set himself, however, at once to work to finish his Cathedral and make all the requisite arrangements for its opening on 14th January 1847. He writes: "The chimes of Vulliamy's clock in the Cathedral are beginning to delight all Calcutta. The inscription on the great bell '*Its sound is gone out into all lands*' is to be gilded. This, with 'the arrow of the Lord's deliverance,' will, I hope, prove an

* This was destroyed by the Cyclone of 5th October, 1864.

augury and pledge of the salvation of India." On the 3rd of March, he notices the rejoicings which took place for the victories over the Sikhs. "A temporary arch is reared with the words Aliwal, Moodkee, Sobraon, and Ferozeshuhur on the four sides. The fields of the Esplanade *(maidán)* are crowded with natives, and at one extremity of it stand two hundred and fifty-two Sikh guns. Elephants and camels are crowding in. I had the utmost difficulty in getting through the dense crowd." As the cold weather of 1847 came on, the Cathedral rapidly approached completion, and, on 14th September he writes, "We had our last 'Building Committee' yesterday. I dissolved it and then formed the members into a Cathedral Vestry, to meet for the first time on October 4th, just before the consecration.

Exactly eight years elapsed between the laying of the foundation-stone of St. Paul's Cathedral, and its consecration on 8th October 1847. The expenses of its erection were nearly 5 lakhs of rupees. The intention of Bishop Wilson was, that in addition to its use as a parish church for the Chowringhee district, and as the Metropolitan Cathedral, it should be served by a body of clergy who, under the designation of a Dean and Chapter, should bear a missionary character and carry out missionary objects; but the reluctance of the East India Company to grant an act of incorporation frustrated this part of his design. The excitement and bustle connected with the consecration thoroughly exhausted the Bishop and brought on a fit of illness which happily did not last long, but compelled him to engage a "retreat" at Cossipore, to which he might retire occasionally for air and rest.

On 22nd January 1848, he speaks of having attended Lord Dalhousie's first *levee*, and on the 18th March of taking Archdeacon Dealtry, who had recently returned from an official tour, to introduce him to Lord and Lady Dalhousie. He rejoices to find that Lord Dalhousie seems more inclined to build churches than Lord Hardinge was, but on May 5th he writes, "The Court of Directors have sent out a fierce letter prohibiting any more churches being built."

The heat and rains of 1848 affected him very much. On 28th July he writes, "I am very old, very peevish, very fractious, very touchy, and though I strive against these infirmities, yet they pervade my conversation and letters I fear more than I am aware of. Forgive me! They are the old man's sins and snares. Dr. Webb is not sorry to see a touch of gout as a safety-valve. I have my great chair with four staves to be carried about the house—a hand-carriage to be drawn about the grounds—my flannel shoe to enable me to walk from room to room." The Doctor pressed him to leave Bengal in the ensuing cold weather, so he made arrangements for his 2nd Metropolitical Visitation, delivered his 5th Charge, and then set out accompanied by his Domestic Chaplain, Mr. Pratt, in the Pilot brig *Tavoy*, Captain Hand, for Bombay, which he reached after a pleasant voyage on 4th December 1848. Lord Falkland the Governor of Bombay, Bishop Carr, and the Clergy welcomed him kindly, and he was able to perform all the duties required of him, but he complains that he was "a good deal whirled about," and that "he had no Dr. Webb to look after him." While hastening in a small steamer to join the *Tavoy* which had left previously, he fell, while walking incautiously, down an open hatchway, but having happily lighted on his feet, escaped with no further injury than a most severe shaking and a livid bruise all down his thigh. Colombo was reached on 29th December. On 5th January 1849 he delivered his Charge, the new Bishop of

Colombo preaching the sermon. On 1st February he arrived at Madras. He was courteously received by the Governor, Sir H. Pottinger, who sent an Aide-de-camp to see him over the surf. Bishop Spencer had retired from the See on the plea of ill-health, so he took up his quarters with Archdeacon Shortland. Nine sermons and addresses, an ordination and the delivery of his Charge quite exhausted his strength. He was attacked with low fever and obliged to be hurried off to sea, leaving a confirmation for which all preparations had been made, unperformed. He reached Calcutta on 2nd March. On the 23rd March the first hint is given of the change of the palace from Russell-street to Chowringhee-road. "We have been," he says, "to inspect Mr. Wilberforce Bird's late house in the Chowringhee-road, which I am advised to make the Bishop's Palace instead of the one which they have inhabited here for 18 years. The advantages are, its immediate vicinity to the Cathedral—a more airy situation—and ground near, which will suit for *schools* and *missionaries'* houses."

On 31st March he writes, "The war is over and the Punjab is annexed. It will be placed under Sir Henry Lawrence, a most admirable and pious man, with E. Thornton, Macleod, Montgomery, and Pearson, all able and well disposed. Surely I shall soon have a Bishop of Agra! for Chaplains will be planted all over the newly-acquired territories with the army and civilians." Lord Dalhousie intimated his wish for a Thanksgiving service on the occasion of the termination of the war. The Bishop gave the order, and himself preached at the Cathedral on the Thanksgiving-day, 6th May 1849. His sermon on the occasion together with that preached after the victory of Guzerat, he printed and circulated. Though such exercises were evidently now a burden to him, for he writes, "I feel quite relieved now that these sermons are done. I fully resolve to print no more."

On 21st September 1849, he resumed his Visitation, by going up to Allahabad by the river, stopping on his way down again at all the various stations *en route*, and arriving again in Calcutta on 22nd January 1850.[1] During this period, Dr. Kay arrived as new Principal of Bishop's College, and Archdeacon Dealtry having been promoted to the See of Madras, Mr. Pratt was made Archdeacon of Calcutta. On arriving in Calcutta, the Bishop took up his quarters at the new palace.

The Lent Lectures this year on the "Christian Armour" were delivered at the Old Church. On 19th April 1850, he writes the Act for the establishment of Liberty of Conscience here passed on April 11th. This will be as memorable a day as December 14th, 1829, when Lord William Bentinck abolished the rite of *suttee*. Now the Hindu or Mahometan who may embrace the Christian faith will no longer forfeit his inheritance.

On 5th August 1850, the Bishop started for Dacca and Assam, Gowhatti, Dibroghur, Tezpore or the City of Blood, and Seebsaugor were all visited, and on the return voyage Mymensing, Burrisaul and Culneah. Most of these stations had never been visited before. On his return to Calcutta on 20th September 1850, he found his new Domestic Chaplain, Rev. J. Bloomfield, arrived. Having received a request from the Bishop of London, that he should visit Borneo on 11th November 1850, he started for Burmah and the Straits, reaching the mouth of the Sarawak River after various difficulties from the roughness of the weather on 18th January 1851. Sir James Brooke unfortunately being ill with fever and not expecting the Bishop, had left for Singapore, where they afterwards met. Mr. Macdoughall however, the future Bishop of Labuan, received the Bishop in his house. The Church, built of *iron-wood* and palm, was consecrated. Various services were held, and on the 23rd January, he set off for Singapore again, which he reached on the 25th January "exhausted and pale as ashes." On his return voyage, he touched again at some of the places at which he had already called, and visited Pooree and Cuttack; and on the 14th March 1851, arrived again in Calcutta. In the following month he was suddenly summoned by a letter from Dr. Kay to attend the death-bed of Mr. Street, the Junior Professor at Bishop's College. Mr. Street appears to have been a true man of God, "an Israelite indeed in whom is no guile." He died on the 29th April and was buried in the little cemetery attached to the College, the Bishop reading the funeral service.

On the 4th June, Bishop Wilson was attacked with an illness which assumed a most serious form, and finally became chronic, rendering him liable to dangerous seizures at any moment and requiring occasional surgical relief to the end of his life. He therefore gave the Archdeacon a commission to visit the Upper Provinces in his stead, and remained quietly in Calcutta until the period for the delivery of his next Charge came round. This Charge (his sixth) was delivered on 1st October 1851. It was like his previous ones very plain spoken and decided in tone, and so he wished it to be, for when an edition of it in England was called for, he wrote to his son "Don't tinker it, don't leave out such plain words as *shuffle*." On 3rd March 1852, he records in his diary the sudden death of Mr. Weitbrecht of Burdwan from cholera, and on 7th April the loss of Mr. Weidemann, Professor at Bishop's College, by drowning, the boat in which he was returning from Howrah to the college having been upset by a North-wester. In the December of 1852 and January of 1853, Dr. Smith, the first Bishop of Victoria, Hong-Kong, paid him a month's visit on his way to China.

During the year 1854 there is very little to record of the Bishop's doings. He managed, however, in the course of it to visit Krishnaghur and Burdwan, and to get up the river in the autumn as far as Allahabad on an episcopal tour, returning by the same route. The following well-known lines, however, of the unfortunate Mary Queen of Scots, which he says that Mr. Boswell had brought him, express his condition all about this time extremely well.

(O Domine Deus speravi in Te)
O care mi Jesu nunc libera me
In dura catena
In misera pœna
Flendo gemendo
Et genu flectendo
Adoro imploro
Ut liberes me.

On 5th February 1855, he mentions the inauguration on the previous Saturday of the East Indian Railway. On the arrival of the Governor-General he says, "I read a prayer in my Church Robes before the train started, and Mr. Fisher who was acting as Archdeacon, and Mr. Bloomfield, his Domestic Chaplain, read some portions of Holy Scripture." On 31st March, 1855, he writes, "Mrs. Ellerton came to reside with me (as house-keeper), on the 27th. She enters her 84th year on May 30th. She is very chatty and pleasant and punctual in coming to meals. . . . . . She has a turn for humour and tells anecdotes of former times. She jokes with me and calls me *twice seven* (77)." This Mrs. Ellerton remained with the Bishop till his death, and only survived him three weeks.

On the 22nd October, he records the consecration by himself, Bishop Dealtry of Madras, and Bishop Smith of Victoria Hong-Kong, of Dr. Macdoughall as Bishop of Borneo. On 23rd October 1855, he delivered his 7th and last Charge and then set off in the *Tenasserim* for Burmah. At Rangoon, he met Lord Dalhousie and found him willing to fall in with all his plans. The foundation-stone of a new Church in the town of Rangoon was laid, to be called St. Andrew's, "in reverence and gratitude for Andrew, Marquis Dalhousie." Another Church also was planned for cantonments. He then having visited and admired the American Missions to the Karens at Kemendine, went 400 miles up the Irawaddy to Thyet Myoo, and advancing ten miles beyond it to the frontier line and mounting the three steps of the flag-staff pillar of demarcation, he looked towards the Burmese side and said "we bless Thee and praise Thee, O Lord, for the tranquillity granted to this land, and we pray that the light of Thy blessed Gospel may be diffused throughout it."

From Burmah, he returned to Calcutta, and then paid a short visit to Madras and Ceylon, meeting at Galle Lord and Lady Canning on their way to Calcutta, whither by April 23rd, 1856, he had himself returned. On 22nd December, he had a fall in his verandah, which fractured the upper part of one of his thigh-bones in the socket. It was set with great skill and care by Dr. Webb, and though now in his 80th year, he recovered his usual measure of health. The early part of 1857 was occupied with a good deal of correspondence with people of influence at home with a view to the securing of a Coadjutor-Bishop. But the plan, as interfering with the patronage of the Prime-minister, very naturally fell through, and as the year went on all thoughts were of necessity centered upon the horrors of the Indian Mutiny. The Bishop was in his house at Serampore when it first broke out, and remained there long after he had been warned by officers who had the best means of information that his life was in the most imminent peril in such an unguarded spot. At last towards the end of June he retired to Calcutta. In the midst of the crowds of fugitives who were then collected there the Bishop's heart never quailed or failed; he maintained that it was a crisis not a catastrophe—a time to humble our souls before God, but by no means to despair, and he closed his long and faithful pulpit ministrations by a sermon on the present state of India from Hab. 1-12: "Art not thou from everlasting, O LORD my GOD, mine Holy one? We shall not die O LORD: Thou hast ordained them for judgment, and O mighty GOD thou hast established them for correction."

We have now reached the closing scenes of Bishop Wilson's career. His "Humiliation Sermon" as it was called, was dedicated to Lord Canning, and, accompanied by a short pastoral address, printed and circulated. On the arrival of Captain Peel in the *Shannon*, with his famous Naval Brigade, the Bishop, at Captain Peel's invitation went on board, and, after having had them marshalled and marched past him, addressed a few words to them, recommending religion as the one thing needful, and exhorting them to go forth and do their part in the deliverance of India. The effect of the publication of the Bishop's sermon was soon felt, and though rather late in the day, Government, in answer to a numerously-signed memorial, proclaimed a day for a national fast and service connected therewith. The Bishop proposed all the necessary forms and issued the requisite notices, but he was too ill to preach or take any part in the services. A trip to sea was recommended and, accompanied by Dr. Webb, he set out in the *Francis Gordon* steamer for the Sandheads. But duty pursued him even here. The *Francis Gordon* was recalled to attend on the *Sanspareil,* a screw 3-decker of 72 guns, which had been diverted on the emergency from her course China-wards to Calcutta. The Captain of the *Sanspareil* came on board and asked the Bishop to address his men. He was accordingly hoisted on board being in such a feeble state as to be quite incapable of walking, and addressed the men for sometime with great earnestness and power.

The constant requisition of the steamer in which he was for the public service, prevented the Bishop from ever getting to sea, and he derived no benefit from being on board. It was determined, therefore, that he should go for sea-air to to the Pilot Vessel at the mouth of Hooghly. He accordingly went there on December 14th, 1857, and spent 14 days on board. At first he seemed to rally, but on the 27th he was attacked with fever, and a return to Calcutta was determined upon. On the Sunday night he had the misfortune to fall out of his cot, though fortunately without any apparent damage.

On the following day the steamer *Harbinger* from Madras having come up, the Bishop was put on board, accompanied by his Chaplain Mr. Walters. At 3 o'clock the steamer reached Calcutta, and he was borne with all possible care and expedition to the palace. Dr. Webb recognized in his symptoms an attack of *Pericarditis* of a rheumatic or gouty character. The Archdeacon, his Chaplain, and Dr. Webb were untiring in their attendance upon him. But as he said "the machine was worn out, the old castle-walls were trembling to their fall." He sunk gradually and almost imperceptibly, till at last in the early morning of 2nd January 1858, just after having taken from the hands of his faithful sirdâr-bearer his usual morning cup of tea, he quickly expired. His departure was so noiseless, that for some little time his servants, who were waiting and watching at the door, were quite unaware of it, supposing him to be asleep. At last, struck by the unusual stillness they became alarmed, and one of them ran to summon Archdeacon Pratt. Hurrying to the bedside he found the Bishop lying calm and apparently unconscious, and hastened to offer up the commendatory prayer in the Prayer-book service for the visitation of the sick. He then sought for any lingering signs of life, but none appeared. Without a struggle or a sigh the spirit had departed to its eternal rest.

With a view to make all the necessary arrangements for his interment in the vault at the east end of his Cathedral, the funeral was deferred for two days. At 4 o'clock on 4th January 1858, his remains were carried by 12 picked men of H. M.'s *Hotspur* to their last resting-place. The Governor-General, the Lieutenant-Governor, the Members of Council, the Judges of the Supreme Court, the Secretaries, many Civil and Military Officers, almost all the clergy and missionaries, and a large concourse of people of all classes attended the funeral. The Archdeacon was chief mourner. The Cathedral Chaplains performed the funeral service.

According to the terms of his will a plain tablet was placed on the east wall of St. Paul's Cathedral and of Bishop's College Chapel, simply recording his name, time of birth, and period that he was Vicar of Islington, and Bishop of Calcutta, and date of his death *and nothing more*, and under this the following words :—

ὁ Θεὸς ἱλάσθητί μοι τῷ ἁμαρτωλῷ

(God be merciful to me, a sinner.)

He left to the Bishop and Archdeacon for the time being, all his books, deposited in the Cathedral and the palace, numbering more than eight thousand, for the use of St. Paul's Cathedral for ever, and he also left to his successors, the Bishops of Calcutta, his iron chest, silver plate, plated-ware, linen, china, glass, household furniture, carriages, and robes of office, to be had at pleasure and handed down in succession.

Such is a brief outline of the life and death of one with whose opinions, if we do not altogether agree, or all of whose acts if we do not approve, we cannot hesitate to pronounce him a king and leader among men. It might perhaps in some respects have been as well for himself, as well as for his diocese, if he could have seen his way to retiring a little earlier from the scene of his labours ; for, during the last ten years of his life he was so feeble and so encompassed with sickness and infirmity, as to be quite incapable of carrying out properly the more active duties of his office. We cannot, however, but sympathize with his noble and manly resolve to stick by India to the last, and leave his bones in that land to which for more than a quarter of a century he consecrated all his energies. Nor must it be supposed when he was laid up from the work of his tours, that he was idle or unoccupied, for he read unceasingly and appreciatingly the literature of the day in its every department, and he took care to express upon it his judgments and criticisms as he proceeded ; which are often most terse, witty and pungent. We have often been amused when turning over the pages of some of his books in the Cathedral Library at the marginal notes, which he has appended *calamo currente* as he went along, and we could have given from the pages of his biography copious quotations of his criticisms, well worthy of record, if we had space for them. Almost on the very day before his death, his bearer had brought him the last new book he had received, a volume of "Livingstone's Travels," and although he found himself quite unequal to the task of perusing it, he managed to glance at it sufficiently to express the opinion upon it to the Archdeacon that "it was a first rate book and by a first rate man." The originality of his character is evidenced by the large number of anecdotes which are told about him in almost every quarter that he visited. Some of them depict him as rather blunt and rude, and as having the knack of saying awkward things in by no means the pleasantest way. Some of them again depict him as dictatorial, egotistic, self-opinionated, and impatient of any thing like counter-argument or contradiction.

It must be allowed we think that he was at times considerably eccentric, and that especially in his later years he carried some of his eccentricities with him into the pulpit to the amusement rather than the edification of his hearers, but after all he must be a very jaundice-eyed critic who does not find in his conduct and conversation far more that he may admire and imitate, than that he may laugh at or condemn, and many a long day may pass over India before she meet with another prelate who shall leave behind him when his biography comes to be written, so many monuments of his energy, his piety, his courage, his diligent studiousness, his simple faith, his unbounded spirit of unstinting and profuse liberality, his willing devotion of every talent and faculty that he possessed to the cause of the Great Master and His Spouse the Church.

LIVES

OF

THE BISHOPS OF CALCUTTA.

COTTON.

George Edward Lynch Cotton was born in 1813, at Chester, at the residence of his grandmother who was the widow of Dr. Cotton, Dean of the cathedral there. A few days after his birth, his father, Captain Cotton, was killed in the battle of the Nivelle, and his education and early training devolved entirely upon his mother and paternal relatives. From his mother he seems to have inherited those literary and intellectual tastes which he never lost, and from his father's family that quaint and grotesque humour for which he was always so remarkable.

Early in 1825, he entered Westminster school and was made a foundationer there in 1828. At school he was chiefly remarkable for his insatiable reading habits, for his 'Socratic irony' and for his kindness to the fags and little boys. He had no taste for cricket, hockey or any kind of athletic sport. He acted twice in the Westminster Plays, and distinguished himself specially on one occasion in the character of an old nurse in the '*Eunuchus*.' The moral tone of the school was as low as that of the general run of public schools at that period, and it is no slight credit to Cotton that it is recorded of him by a contemporary that he always "said his prayers at night."

In 1832, he went up to Trinity College, Cambridge, as a Westminster scholar. His former schoolfellows seem here to have considerably interfered with his studious habits, and he mentions that on one occasion when he had invited a number of them to breakfast at his rooms and had purchased for their special benefit and use a bran new box of cigars, of which he himself never partook, how they entirely disconcerted all his plans of reading for the day by remaining puffing away until Hall-time, a course of action on their part upon which he had not at all calculated.

The religious bent and character of his mind was shown at this period by his becoming a teacher in the Jesus Lane Sunday School, by his joining various religious societies among the undergraduates, and by his professing himself an avowed follower of the Evangelical school, not that he was altogether satisfied with it, but because it was at that time in the University the only religious school that there was to follow. His great Christian hero both at this early period and ever afterwards, was Arnold, and he formed firm and lasting friendships with several of his pupils who were up at the time, such as Charles Vaughan and W. J. Conybeare, Howson, Freeman, and others.

One of his amusements was to draw up a Tripos list of his friends and assign them their several places according to all the rules and niceties of the University Calendar with which he prided himself upon a thorough and perfect acquaintance. He always gained a first class year by year in the college examinations, obtained a declamation prize, and also a prize for reading in chapel which shows that he must have been throughout his career a steady man.

In 1836, he took his B.A. degree graduating as a senior optime and eighth in the first class of the classical Tripos. After this he continued in residence, reading for a Fellowship, which he obtained in due course, and taking pupils, and in the society of such friends as Vaughan and Conybeare, no doubt thoroughly enjoying that most agreeable part of an academic career at Cambridge,—the life of a bachelor-scholar at Trinity.

In the same year he was through Vaughan's influence appointed by Dr. Arnold to a mastership and boarding house at Rugby. Here he remained for 15 years; for the first twelve under Dr. Arnold, and for the last three under his successor Dr. Tait. With the former he lived in the most familiar and friendly intercourse, and most materially assisted him in raising the school to that high standard to which it gradually attained. The readers of "Tom Brown" will remember the allusion which it contains to an under-master who had such a wonderful knack of gaining the confidence of the boys and influencing them in all their doubts and difficulties for good. That master was Cotton.

It was during his life at Rugby, that he compiled those manuals of devotion, confirmation, &c., for school-boys which many have found so useful in the training of children of the upper and better educated order, and that industry and diligence which was so strongly characteristic of him to the end, enabled him to accomplish an astonishing amount of private reading and of correspondence with old friends and old pupils in addition to his regular and carefully performed scholastic duties.

In the year 1845, he married his cousin Sophia Anne Tomkinson, eldest daughter of the Rev. Henry Tomkinson of Reaseheath in Cheshire. On the death of Arnold in 1849, he became, after sundry misgivings as to the propriety of such a course when he had failed in obtaining "*Birmingham*" the year before, a candidate for the head-mastership of Rugby. He says playfully in a letter to a friend that he saw some reasons which seemed to make him fitter for the "*Burmese*" than the Rugbeian empire, but the die was cast and he had determined to stand. Dr. Tait, however, was Arnold's successor, and we have a proof of the completeness with which Cotton won his confidence by his pressing him so earnestly as he did a few years afterwards to abandon his work at Marlborough for the still more important duties of the See of Calcutta.

At last in 1852, he met with a post well calculated to try his calibre and to bring out all his energies. Marlborough, which had been founded in 1843 with such high hopes and on such philanthropic principles as an institution where the sons of the clergy might have all the benefits presented by a thoroughly good public school, was vacant. It had hitherto proved a most disastrous failure. The boys were low-lived and insubordinate, the exchequer was empty and the numbers were falling off, and it appeared as if a total break-up were not far to follow. Some one was required to raise and change the whole character of the school or it must inevitably perish. Those who knew him said 'Cotton is the man!' and so accordingly Cotton was appointed and the school was saved. His popularity with his old pupils gradually drew around him a staff of teachers all imbued with his spirit for earnest Christian work. By this new element whatever was utilizable in the old Marlburian stock was leavened and quickened. The boys were reclaimed from their poaching and poultry stealing and general rebelliousness and after six years that which, when he took it in hand, was almost a *corpus mortuum* had become under his paternal rule a flourishing and vigorous community, full of order, energy, public spirit, high hopes and anticipations of a career of honour and distinction.

The Bishop's appointment to the See of Calcutta took place in 1858, after he had been at Marlborough six years. We ought to have mentioned that in the intervals of his school-work, both at Rugby and Marlborough, he paid several visits to the Continent, and penned from various foreign places in Germany, Italy, France and Spain, letters to his relatives and friends at home in his peculiarly graphic and comically jocose style. Of these the following extract from a letter, dated Gibraltar, February 7th, 1851, may serve as a specimen :—" Here (at Grenada) I had a truly *hair-breadth* escape so marvellous that I can hardly realize it. In the diligence office, when I was taking places for Malaga, I met a certain native of Gibraltar, whom I had previously seen at Seville and who was travelling as a guide to some English officers. He was displaying his musket, which he had just brought to protect his party from robbers, and which he told Blake was loaded with two balls, but said was not cocked. In this belief he pulled the trigger in a swaggering way; the gun instantly went off so close to my head that it actually singed my hair; then it smashed in all the window panes, one ball passing through the frame. Providentially it killed no one in the street, but of course brought half Grenada into and around the office. Had I been standing a single inch to the left of my actual position, the balls must have lodged in my head. The culprit was seized by the police, but released on paying for the damage actually done."

His correspondence with his various friends and former pupils about this time is especially interesting when it alludes to the sceptical tone of thought which had become so fashionable. With this mental malady he was from his fair, cautious and unimpulsive temperament peculiarly well a qualified to cope. When dealing with any doubt or difficulty he always argues the point temperately, considerately, and convincingly on the Christian side, winding up with such weighty words as the following :—" No doubt to reconcile modern thought with Christian faith may be a hard matter of practice, but it is only a repetition of the problem which other ages have successfully solved, and by way of beginning the solution let us hold fast to Christian love and all Christian virtue." Many a soul was saved from sad ship-wreck of its faith through these communications.

Upon the promotion of Dr. Tait to the See of London in 1856, Cotton was chosen to preach his consecration sermon, and in the following year was appointed his examining chaplain in connection with the University of Cambridge. An official connexion was thus re-established between them, and upon the news of the death of Bishop Wilson arriving in England, early in 1858, Dr. Tait, without consulting Cotton, strongly urged upon the Government the advisability of appointing him to the vacant post. Government at first seems to have had some one else in view, but eventually intimation was conveyed to Dr. Tait, that if Dr. Cotton would take the post, it was at his disposal. A telegram was immediately despatched to Marlborough. It found Cotton quietly engaged at his usual duties, and also informed him that he must make up his mind within 24 hours. The cause of this was that the Ministry was just going out and the present Secretary for India, Lord Lyveden, was only holding office till a new Cabinet was formed. Cotton hurried up to town to consult an old friend (Dean Stanley) who strongly urged him to accept the post as being one (1) "who could understand the old religions of India, and (2) could deal fairly and kindly by the different Christian communities." Having made up his mind for acceptance he called the next day on the Indian Minister, who reassured him by the words "I believe that in appointing you I have done the best for the interests of India, of the Church of England, and of Christianity."

His consecration took place in Westminster Abbey upon Ascension Day, his friend, Dr. Vaughan, preaching the sermon; and as it was considered unadvisable for him to leave England before the autumn, he returned for some space to his work at Marlborough, preparing himself quietly in the meantime by the study of the Indian languages and in other ways for his future career. Having appointed by special privilege, accorded to him *honoris causâ*, his successor in office (Dr. Bradly) and having paid a few farewell visits he took final leave of Marlborough early in September. Late in the night of the eve of his departure, he read over with an old friend the 17th chapter of St. John's gospel, and joined with him in prayer. On the following morning, amidst the cheers of the boys, he left for town, and on the 25th September, in company with Mrs. Cotton, his son and little daughter and his future domestic chaplain Mr. Burn, he embarked at Southampton for India.

From this point in Bishop Cotton's life we have in addition to his varied letters and correspondence, the advantage of what he calls "a regular journal of his Indian Episcopate," which was kept by him with the most careful regularity under all difficulties hereafter. The extracts which are found in his Biography from this record are copious, and carry us along most agreeably wherever he goes with himself as our guide upon the way.

Several *last things* in England struck him as solemn and appropriate. "My *last* sermon," he says, "was to the Augustinians, the students of a college from which may flow, I trust, many blessings to India. My *last* regular Sunday service was in Canterbury Cathedral, the birth-place of English Christianity, and endeared to me privately by the thought of Stanley. My *last* service of any kind was in Westminster Abbey, where I worshipped in boyhood, and where I was consecrated to the office of Bishop. My *last* visit was to Weybridge to the grave of dear Conybeare, my closest and, in one sense, my oldest friend. We were accompanied to the steamer at Southampton by friends and relations of many ages and representing different classes of valued intimacies and close ties; and though these partings were full of sorrow yet we separated, not, I trust, as those who have no hope, but in the belief that we are in the hands of a loving Father, whose tenderness has not failed us in time past and will not fail us in times to come."

On 9th October 1858 he was at Cairo and witnessed the ceremomy of the presentation to the Pasha of Egypt of the *Mahmel* or sacred canopy, which during the previous year had been placed over the Kaaba at Mecca. Of the Pasha and his court, the many-uniformed troops, the Bedouin horsemen in their national costume, the fanatical Mahomedans, the representative of their prophet's family, the pilgrims, the music, the presenting arms, the pipes, cymbals and kettledrums, and the thoroughly strange mixture of

Western and Eastern pomp and parade at a great Islamic festal display, he gives a most amusing description. He seems to have stayed at Cairo about ten days, visiting on the 13th October the Armenian Patriarch (who said "that he embraced in brotherly communion all episcopal churches, Greek, Syrian, Coptic, English, &c., except the Roman on account of its claims to universal authority and exclusive salvation);" and on the 18th October two Coptic Churches in old Cairo, one of them built over a cave in which the Holy Family are said to have lived.

Just before leaving Cairo he enjoyed the opportunity of witnessing the extraordinary and revolting ceremony of the *Doseh*, with which, he says, is concluded a kind of fair which has been held in the Uzbekieh (a large square in the middle of Cairo) ever since the return of the pilgrims from Mecca, in honour of the prophet's birth day. The proceedings took place at the house of Sheykh el-Bekir said to be descended from the Khalif Abu Bekir and the head of Mahomedanism in Egypt. Here various Europeans and native dignitaries were assembled, and the main part of the spectacle is described as follows :—"After a long delay we went into the Court which was nearly filled with dervishes, pilgrims, policemen, soldiers, and spectators. A space was cleared in the middle and in rushed a tumultuous crowd, shrieking and struggling, some with drums and cymbals. Some of these threw themselves on the ground and were arranged on their stomachs in a regular line along the open space; any who were not quite straight were pulled into order, and there was a furious uproar about setting them near the entrance of the Court, vehement use of the bamboo, kicking, pummelling and shouting. At last in walked some attendants over these prostrate devotees, then two men bearing enormously high green poles surmounted by crescents; amidst a Babel of frantic fanaticism, the Sheykh of a certain set of dervishes (the Sáadéeh) rode over them on a horse led by two grooms. The confusion at the end was indescribable. I thought the horse and the green poles were coming full tilt against the spectators."

No accident however happened. The Sheykh dismounted, and the devotees, though in some cases horribly bruised, got up and shook themselves. Then came more howling and roaring and strange antics on the part of dervishes and devotees and rewarding of some of them with yellow and pink robes. "The great use of seeing such an exibition," he says. "is that it entirely dispels the notion that Mahomedanism is a calm and contemplative religion of common sense; For even Hindu orgies cannot be much wilder than the *Doseh,* though it is now exhibited in a mitigated form and divested of its old accompaniments of dervishes tearing serpents to pieces with their teeth and thrusting red-hot daggers into their bodies, or of men who had taken a vow never to wash, dancing bedaubed with mire, all of which additions were practised within recent times."

On Oct. 27th he arrived at Aden and on 5th Nov. at Galle, where a kind of preliminary installation of him as Metropolitan was held in the old Dutch Church and an address presented to him by the Bishop and Clergy of the diocese of Colombo. On the 8th November he was at Madras where great rejoicings and illuminations were in progress on account of the transfer of the Government of India to the Crown; and on the 12th November the *Candia* was off Saugor Island which he describes as "a low, woody, frowzy looking swamp, abandoned to jungle, fevers, tigers and light-house men, the last being protected from the second by barricades and entrenchment, and he supposes accustomed to the 'first." Archdeacon Pratt met him at the Garden Reach Ghat on the following day, and conducted him to his new home which he entered with prayers and thanksgivings and fervent aspirations that it might be a centre of light in a dark land. On Sunday, 14th November, he was installed in the cathedral of which he praises the spire, the chimes, and the green compound, but complains that it is too like a great hall inside.

The labour and responsibility of the See of Calcutta had been most materially reduced by the growth of the Colonial Episcopate during the time of Bishop Wilson. Madras, Bombay, Borneo and the Straits, which alone of H. M. Eastern possessions it had been usual for the Bishop of Calcutta to visit in person, as well as other places further off, over which his nominal authority extended, each had now their own Bishop. Still, however, British Burmah and the vast Presidency of Bengal presented a field of sufficiently varied and ample Diocesan proportions, and if Bishop Cotton's mission therein was, as Dr. Vaughan had described it in his consecration sermon, "to quicken the energies and regulate the labours of missionaries of Christ in the East and to build up again from its ruins a Church desolate and distressed and baptized in blood," there was evidently work enough before him to tax every faculty both of body and mind. He spent his first ten months of Indian life in Calcutta and the neighbourhood; getting up gradually, at head-quarters, the business of his Diocese; learning Bengali and Urdu, visiting some of the Church Missionary Society's stations at Krishnagur, Burdwan, &c. (which he describes as wonderfully like parishes in England with church parsonage and schools in good order, but hardly sufficiently aggressive upon the domain of heathenism around them). And especially during the summer months superintending the delivery by himself and others of a course of lectures to educated native young men. The subjects were—

1.—Lessons suggested by the Early History of India.

2.—St. Augustine (of Africa.)

3.—The Emperor Julian.

4.—The Institutes of Menu (the Hindu Lawgiver) and Education.

5.—Dr. Arnold.

He describes the lecture on St. Augustine which was given by Dr. Kay as "extremely interesting, most graceful and touching in its language, and exceedingly well adapted to the Bengalis, who at the end applauded it in a manner which, for their lazy temperaments, may be called vociferous." He mentions that some official had objected to the use of the Medical College Theatre in Calcutta for the lectures, fearing that they might have a missionary tendency, and that his scruples had caused considerable amusement to some of the young men themselves who thought that they might have been credited with intelligence sufficient to be aware that they were not going to be instructed in Christianity in their Theatre as they were in medicine or anatomy.

We mentioned that almost the last thing which Bishop Wilson did for the diocese, was to preach and publish his 'Humiliation Sermon,' which was followed not long after by a Government order for a day of general fasting and prayer on account of the 'war and tumults' of the mutiny. The last expiring scintillations of the great conflagration still lingered in Oudh and Berar when Bishop Cotton reached the shores of India, and it was not till after he had been in the country about nine months that he had the happy privilege of being able to write to his friend Dr. Vaughan the following words :—"We had our thanksgiving day on July 28th (1859). It went off I hope well. The Governor-General and Council came to the Cathedral in state and took part in the service drawn up by me, and listened with decorous attention to my discourse."

Among other matters of interest in his journal and diary at this period, we may be permitted, perhaps, briefly to notice a few particulars.

In the month of February at a dinner party, he had the great pleasure of meeting the British officer's model and the British soldier's idol—Sir James Outram, with whom he evidently had one of those long, interesting and congenial talks which he so thoroughly enjoyed. Sir James, he says, spoke of his soldiers with the greatest affection; highly commended the services of the chaplains on various occasions; lamented the blood-thirstiness of the English during the mutiny and rejoiced that he had never hung a sepoy; attributed the revolt to a temporary madness; admired the Queen's proclamation, and considered that the whole effect would be to deal a severe blow to Brahminism and to promote Christianity, to which sentiment there is the very proper subscription *Faxit Deus!*

In March he sent home his son under charge of Mr. Spry, the exellent Chaplain of Allahabad, who, he says, remained bravely in the midst of his flock through the mutiny, and will, he has no doubt, take as good care of his son as he did of them.

In a letter to Arthur Watson, Esq., dated 1st May 1859, he says of Positivism that it teaches no moral truths, but such as Christianity has taught, if rightly understood, for the last eighteen centuries, and that as it brings us nothing fresh and requires us to throw away so much that is valuable, there should be no dallying with it!

In a letter to Mrs. Arnold, dated 31st May 1859, he writes in a manner which must have been indeed precious to the bereaved mother's heart regarding the death of her gifted son "Willy," who after running such a brief but brilliant career as a School Inspector in the Punjab, died at sea on his way home. He seems in the conversations which he had with Bishop Cotton at the Palace shortly before he embarked to have expressed a desire for some fresh evidence of Christianity which should clear away difficulties relating to inspiration. "But after all" the Bishop writes—he said "there was no difficulty greater than to believe that the sermon on the Mount was not Divine."

We now return to the chronological course of events. The primary Charge was delivered in September 1859. Its principal subject was, "the relation in which the Government of India stands to Christianity, especially with reference to education." The topic at the time was on every tongue both in England and India in consequence of the new relations into which India had recently been brought to the British crown and of Lord Stanley's famous educational dispatch of 1859. "The Bishop begins by expressing his regret at an opinion which had been maintained in a Report of Public Instruction, that Government had no connection whatever with Christianity, and that it was as unmeaning to talk of a Christian Government as it would be to talk of a Christian system of police or a Christian system of roads and canals." He replies that if by the latter is meant the actual material system of roads, then as a road has not conscience and reason it cannot be compared with a society of thinking and responsible agents; but if the Commissioners or Company, who manage the roads are meant, then as such a body is not invested with the sovereign attributes of capital punishment, making war and exercising absolute uncontrolled authority, it cannot afford any guide to the functions of a body possessed with powers which seem to be entrusted to it for the highest and not merely for the lowest good of men.

Again he objects to the word *neutrality* as used in describing the relation of the British Government to religion, and says, "nor can I ever hear it without thinking of our Lord's warning, He that is not with me, is against me! It is impossible for any thoughtful man to be really indifferent to the contest between two such principles as Christianity and Heathenism, nor in truth can we claim to have been so when we have taken upon ourselves to decide that certain parts of the Hindu system are immoral and to prohibit them by law."

The Bishop then contrasts our present position in India with that of our predecessors. He reminds us that in 1812, a missionary to British India could find no rest for the sole of his foot except in the Danish settlement of Serampore, or the heathen kingdom of Ava, and he reminds us that even Lord Stanley the very minister whose very deeds and words had been so severely criticised as hostile to the spread of Christianity in India had actually ordered the gradual but speedy suppression of the cruelties practised at the *Charak Poojah* had forbidden the executive to superintend the fulfilment of trusts for idolatrous purposes, and had refused to recognize heathenism in the Courts of Justice by the forms of administering oaths." "We can now plant missions," he adds, "all over the country, when and where we will, we can obtain Government help for schools in which the Bible is taught to every scholar, we can bring our books and our teaching to bear on every class of the population."

He then states it as his opinion that practical difficulties make it for the present impossible that the introduction of the Bible into Government schools should be a measure of much real importance; he deprecates anything like a compulsory attendance on Bible classes in Government schools, and speaks warmly in favour of a more extended education in the vernacular as the best preparation for the Gospel. "To distribute books and tracts," he says "among the ignorant rural population is a mere waste of time and labour, and those who have never been taught to reflect at all can hardly understand why the service of Christ is better than that of Siva or Kali."*

Although the Bishop thus expressed himself against the compulsory system of Bible reading or Bible teaching in the schools, feeling very strongly that it was far better that the Bible should never be seen than that it should be read to and explained by a master who should sneer and cavil at its contents, still it should be known that he made to the Governor-General a strenuous and successful appeal on behalf of voluntary Bible classes in Government buildings. Whether the rule that the Bible in English and the chief vernaculars should be in the library of every Government school is in any way due to Bishop Cotton we cannot say, but it certainly is a rule which would have had his countenance and support.

Immediately after the delivery of his Charge the Bishop left Calcutta for his first up-country tour.

---

* This analysis of the Bishop's primary Charge is taken from a Lecture on Bishop Cotton by the Rev. W. Spencer, Bengal Chaplain.

Our object in giving some account of Bishop Cotton's First Visitation Tour will be—(1) to trace the course of it so far as we can, and to record any of his official acts which appear to have an historical value; (2) to cull from his Diary any remarks upon scenery, places, or people which strike us as entertaining or instructive.

The first part of the journey was accomplished in the barge of the Lieutenant-Governor of Bengal, towed by a Government steamer. The route adopted at the outset was through the Sunderbuns, and as might naturally be expected when the cold weather was only just setting in, the Bishop and his chaplain were both attacked with fever which never left them till after they had been, for some little time, in the North-Western Provinces.

The Bishop entered the North-West Provinces on November 3rd at Buxar, and rather less than a week afterwards he reached Benares. Here he spent several days among the temples and ghats, the monasteries and mosques, the picturesque streets and elegant kiosks, which are spread in such rich profusion throughout the *Athens* of India; and of course he also paid a careful and observant visit to the Church Missionary Society's premises at Sigra and to Jay Narain's College, which is under their superintendence, and to the Government College. The only part of the famous mosque of Aurungzebe which he admires is the two minarets. The Hindu temples, he thinks, far more interesting, specially the famous one of Vishvesheshwara "having a dome covered with gilding, or, as the people say, with gold as thick as an eight-anna-piece." Near to this temple he notices the sacred well "into which the god jumped when the city was taken by the Mussulmans." He also alludes to the vulgar belief that all the stones of Benares are gold, though the fact is at present hidden from mortal eyes, except in the case of Vishveshwara's temple; and expresses considerable admiration of the city as seen from a boat in progress on the river about sunset,—'a sight,' he says, 'much to be remembered, and to be compared with many fine views of European cities. He considers Jay Narain's College, though architecturally unpretending, yet, with its separate class-rooms opening into verandahs, better adapted for its purpose than the '*Gothic aspirations*' of the Government College.

On the 26th November, 1859, the Bishop reached Cawnpore. The state in which he describes it as existing then, so soon after the subsidence of the mutiny, compared with that which it wears now. that it has had time to recover somewhat of its previous aspect, and rejoices in its new memorial church, is deeply interesting.

After his visit to the well now embosomed in a blooming and carefully kept flower-garden and garnished with the handsomest Gothic monument erected by English hands in India, he says 'all traces have vanished of the house in which the massacre took place; but in a wide expanse of sand with a few palm-trees and two European houses near, is the mouth of the well, completely bricked up, rising about a foot from the ground and surrounded by a wooden fence. On one side is the well-known cross put up by the men of the 32nd under Moore's (the chaplain's) auspices; on the other a plain horizontal gravestone with a cross carved upon it and the two texts from Joel ii, 17—'*Spare thy people, O Lord, and give not thine heritage to reproach, that the heathen should rule over them: wherefore should they say among the people, where is their God.*' 21—'*Fear not O land be glad and rejoice, for the Lord will do great things.*' This was put up by a Non-Commissioned Officer of the Bengal Artillery to the women and children belonging to his corps. On the upright cross to the memory of those belonging to the 32nd, the motto is—'*I believe in the Resurrection of the body.*' Surely these are among the most melancholy memorials in the world! &c.'

He then describes '*Wheeler's Entrenchments,*' which were nothing more than a ditch and a parapet drawn round a portion of the military lines, 'the barrack which was occupied till the mutineers set it on fire, the well in which the dead were buried secretly at night by parties who stole out at the peril of their lives to perform the last rites to their comrades,' and then says of the general aspect of Cawnpore,—'In desolation it surpasses any station which we have yet seen' * * * and everything at present looks miserable and depressed, and even the residents seem specially to dislike the place as if the curse of the Nana still blighted it. On the other hand, there is the memory of Henry Martyn to hallow it, while the thoroughly solid and substantial masonry of the Ganges Canal which terminates here and the handsome new railway station, hold out a prospect of future material prosperity.'

On 28th November 1859, the Bishop quitted Cawnpore and arrived on the following day at Lucknow, where the proper occupant being absent on cold weather circuit, the Chief Commisioner's residence, '*Bank's House,*'* once the abode of an Oudh Begum, was placed at his disposal. From the roof of this he describes the view as 'strikingly beautiful; among a great mass of trees there rise in every direction domes and minarets, mosques and palaces, * * * and the whole effect is really fine. He of course visited these after-

* So called from Major Banks who lies buried in the Residency cemetry, close by Sir Henry Lawrence.

wards somewhat in detail. He spent some time in examining the residency, its battered walls, its ruined church, its deeply interesting cemetery, and took a careful survey of the course of the out-works which were defended during the mutiny with such desperate and unflinching pertinacity until Havelock, Outram and Clyde brought relief to the besieged. The remainder of the week was occupied in visiting the C. M. S. Mission and in ministering to the general body of the residents in the Civil Church or to the soldiers in cantonments.

On 6th December 1859, he left Lucknow, and having visited 5 miles on his way, Havelock's grave in the Alumbagh, he again arrived in Cawnpore at 5 o'clock the same evening. Next morning he walked to another fatal spot of sad notoriety, the '*Suttee Chunder Ghât*' (on the Ganges) where the victims of the Nana's shameless falsehood embarked in the boats and were massacred by the cowards who had been unable by fair fighting to conquer such a force in such a fortress as 'Wheeler's Entrenchments.' At four the same afternoon, he held a confirmation—a miserable contrast, he observes, to that at Lucknow.

On 15th December 1859, he reached Agra. Here there was much to be done, for besides the fair and stately fabrics of the fort, the Tajmahal, the Itimad-ud-Dowlah and Akber's Tomb at Secundra, there was an ordination to be held, the C. M. S. College to visit and examine, as well as the C. M. S. Secundra Orphanage now just again beginning to revive from its desolations. We cannot possibly give the Bishop's remarks upon all these points. Into each and all of them he went with his accustomed zeal and interest. All we need say is, knowing as we do something of Agra from personal inspection we can affirm that whoever may visit it will find his *Diary* the very best guide-book that they can take with them for an account of the great monuments of the place. He was much struck with the excellence of the education imparted in the St. John's College (C. M. S.), and he appears to have been equally interested and encouraged by what he saw and took part in, finishing his sojourn by a thoroughly hard day's work on December 25th, Christmas-day, 1859. On the 27th he reached Delhi.

We must not dwell upon the Bishop's description of Shahjehan's capital, thence called in all old documents Shahjehanabad and now Delhi. It is of course lively, picturesque, careful and full of well-digested information culled from every quarter. The Fort, the Cashmere Gate, the site of the English Camp during the mutiny on the heights to the north of the city, Humayon's Tomb and the Tombs of the kings of Delhi which adjoin in, the Mausoleum of Nizam-ud-din, and the Kutb Minar, which he says and its accessories "form the grandest of Delhi sights," all the prominent features in fact of the ruins or of the ancient or modern beauties of the grand old capital are accurately delineated by his untiring pen.

We merely give the following extract from his account of the Church, because it contains his opinion upon painted windows and mural tablets in Churches. After stating that it was intended to erect painted windows to the memory of the Rev. Mr. Jennings and other victims of the mutiny, he writes—"Many persons object to painted windows in Indian churches, when they represent living beings as giving Mahometans a notion that Christianity is an idolatrous religion and would tolerate nothing more than mere kaleidoscope glass, as in Bishop's College Chapel and the transepts of the Cathedral. I think that there is something in the objection in the case of single figures, and that if a Mussulman sáw a large east window, filled with separate representations of the Apostles, he might think that the saints were objects of our worship. But I do not see how he could suspect us of worshipping a group such as that which Bishop Wilson allowed to be placed in the east window of the Cathedral; and, on the other hand, it is important that Christianity should vindicate to itself something more of outward beauty and majesty than it has hitherto admitted in India. Indeed, since the mutiny the desire for memorials in Churches is so general, that to refuse windows will only be to multiply those *hideous tablets which deface our walls.*"

During his stay at Delhi, the Bishop had much interesting conversation with Ram Chundra, a well-educated native convert, "who was reclaimed from philosophical Deism by reading the New Testament and seeing the devout worship of educated Englishmen,—a striking instance of the concurrent evidence of the Gospel and the Church, of Christianity and Christendom."

On 10th January 1860, at Roorkee, the Bishop first saw the Himalayas. "Three ranges," he says, "are distinctly visible—(1) The low outwork of the Sewallic range; (2) The blue hills of Mussoorie, (3) The magnificent snowy mountains standing up against the sky like a gigantic wall with white battlements."

On the 18th January he arrived at Umballa, and encountered the Governor-General (Lord Canning) in the progress of his Viceregal tour. On the following day he attended a grand Durbar, which, with all its accompaniments of *nuzzurs* of gold mohurs, trays of shawls, plate and jewels, presented by thin-legged native gentlmen in tights and parti-coloured stockings, *khiluts*, (*i.e*, return-presents from the Governor-

General) and *pawn*, winding up with 'God save the Queen,' he paints to the life.

At the close of his account of his visitation of Umballa, he throws in the following significant remark upon the value of the policy of preserving a territorial native aristocracy in India:—"Lord Canning is plainly anxious to establish or restore in India something of a territorial aristocracy; in Oude this is certainly possible, in the Punjab he hopes so, but in the North-West Provinces he has asked in every district whether there are any natives, influential enough to be entrusted with magisterial powers; but the answer has universally been—No! there is nothing really between the Government and the village communities. The policy has hitherto been to lop off the heads of the tallest poppies, to get rid of those who might possibly recalcitrate against our rule; but it is now discovered that those who might recalcitrate might also be very useful."

On 30th January, passing through Loodiana, he crossed the Sutlej, and entered the Punjab, and travelling by way of Kussoor reached the rich and fertile banks of the Ravee, and entered Lahore late at night. Lahore, he says, may be divided into three component parts,—(1) Anarkalli, the civil station said to be called after a slave girl, the inmate of the harem of a Mogul Emperor; (2) The native city of Lahore; (3) Meean-Meer, the military station, five miles from Anarkalli. Into his account of these we cannot enter further than to remark that on the morning of February 2nd, he visited the 'grand and striking' Mausoleum of Jehanghir at the village of Shadra near Lahore, in reference to which he remarks—"So now I am getting to know—in many cases to have seen—the places of interment of the six great emperors of the house of Timour—Baber at Cabul; Humayon at Delhi; Akbar at Secundra, near Agra; Jehanghir at Shadra near Lahore; Shajehan in the Taj at Agra; Aurangzeb at Aurangabad." In the evening of the same day he went to service and preached in Anarkalli's tomb "which now surmounted by a large cross thirteen feet high, very neatly fitted up and purified from Mussulman worship by the consecration of the Bishop of Madras in 1857, has become St. James's Church.

In connexion with his visit to Meean-Meer, which took effect on 3rd February, he gives the following account of the mode in which he acquired the habit (which, however, he but sparely exercised) of preaching *extempore*, as on this occasion he had just been doing in the Church of S. Mary Magdalene to the soldiers:—"What a comfort it is that I can extemporize with some fluency! *I should be sorry so to use the power as to get careless or lazy about writing sermons*, but the ability to do it seems absolutely necessary to my present office, and is one of the many good things which I learned at Marlborough, where it was necessary sometimes to harangue the school at a moment's notice, especially in the early days when some of them had murdered a dog."

The morning of February 4th was devoted to conversation with various missionaries and to visiting the large American Presbyterian Mission School in Lahore, containing 320 boys. The school he pronounces a good one, but not so good as the C. M. S. St. John's College at Agra. In the evening he rode on an elephant into the town of Lahore, and viewed—(1) the Wuzeeri mosque (which he describes as 'a perfect blaze of colour'); (2) the Padshah's mosque; (3) the Fort; and (4) the tomb of Runjeet Singh. On this he remarks—"As Sikhism is a mixture of Islam and Hinduism, so the body of Runjeet Singh was burnt, and half the ashes thrown into the Ganges, Hindu fashion, while the other half, according to Mahometan practice, were buried under this tomb. But instead of the oblong sarcophagus which marks the resting-place of a Mussulman, the ashes of Runjeet Singh are enclosed in a white marble globe. Around this are the frightful memorials of a horrible superstition. *Eleven smaller globes encircle the great one containing the dust of eleven women, four Ranees and seven slave girls, who were burnt as Suttees with the body of the Rajah.*"

The route which the Bishop followed between Lahore and Rawul Pindee is not stated in his diary, but we may be pretty sure that he travelled by the main road from south-east to north-west and so crossed the river Chenab at Wuzeerabad, and the river Jhelum at the town of Jhelum. He reached Rawul Pindee (lat. 33° 37′ long. 73° 6′) on February 11th, and having spent one day there, proceeded through a rough and wild country encircled by mountains towards Attock. On Tuesday, 14th February, at 1 A.M., 'he heard,' he says, 'the roaring of the Indus *beyond which no Hindu ought to pass.* Some persons suppose that Attock, which signifies '*obstacle*," derives its name from this superstition of the Hindus. Some again think that it is so called because at this point, after receiving the waters of the Cabul river, the Indus first becomes navigable. Some say that the Emperor Akbar gave the name because he found the river here so difficult to cross, and that he formed his fort (which is now adapted to the use of English soldiers) as an additional *obstacle* to would-be invaders of his Indian Empire from the land of the Affghans. The Bishop notices the extreme beauty and picturesqueness of the situation, and says—"We are now at the entrance to Hindustan trodden by Alexander and by the Arab and Tartar invaders. We can appreciate the insufficiency of a river frontier to a great empire, and the necessity of extending the boundary of India to a mountain chain."

Having crossed the Indus and left the picturesque country adjoining it, the Bishop proceeded north-westwards across "a wide, desolate, dusty plain bordered by low hills," till at a distance of 18 miles from Attock he reached the so-called *sanatarium* of Nowshera. It still bore traces of the tremendous inundation of 1856, when a sudden rise in the waters of the Indus dammed up those of the Cabul river, and sent them rolling back in great waves till the whole cantonment was overwhelmed. And the Bishop pronounces it 'the most unhappy-looking of stations !" About 20 more miles brought him into the frontier town of British India and of the Diocese of Calcutta—Peshawur.* Here he found his father's first cousin, General Sir Sydney Cotton, who, from the frequency of his parades and military displays, had, he says, got the nick-name of *Gun-Cotton*, in command.

The Bishop's stay at Peshawur extended over 10 days, and included a variety of work which we need not specify. On February 18th, he consecrated the new Church, though still in an incomplete state. On the 19th he ordained Mr. M'Carthy, C. M. S. Missionary, priest. On the 20th, he made a sort of picnic expedition to the mouth of Khyber Pass *under guard of a very strong escort all armed.* The limit of their expedition was the Fort of Jumrood, 'the very extremity,' the Bishop calls it, 'of English dominion, the frontier of civilization, the mouth of the fatal Khyber Pass.' "The Fort," he says, "is a ruin built on the top

* Peshawur was built by the Moghul Emperor Akbar, and signifies "advanced post."

and up the sides of an isolated hill. From the top is a grand mountain view; the Khyber was just before us, we could trace the winding paths leading up to it, and we could see the tops of the hills bounding the narrow gorge where Sale and his men perished."

On 25th February 1860, the Bishop left Peshawur, and having Simla in view for the hot-weather, began his progress thitherward, taking in his course those stations which lie to the north of the route by which he had come. As far as Rawul Pindee and a little beyond, he seems to have retraced his steps; and Saturday, 10th March, found him at Sealkote. Here he met the Lieutenant-Governor of the Punjab, Sir Robert Montgomery, and went with him to pay a call upon the Rajah of Cashmere, who was encamped there in great state. "As we came up," he says, "the Rajah's band played God save the Queen, in most inharmonious style, and with extraordinary rapidity, the amusing thing being that the perpetrators of this detestable discord say, the English excel the Kashmiris in every thing *except music.*" Of the Maharajah, whom he describes as a young man, very dark, with moustaches twisted into points and turned up in the air; with tunic white and gold, trousers red with yellow spots, turban white, green and gold, neck hung with many rows of large pearls and emeralds, he says "his manners were awkward and his gait slouching like all the native princes I have seen except the Rajah of Jheend. He occupied a chair, opposite the entrance of the tent with sundry ministers and attendant behind him, to whom he kept turning round awkwardly, and asking questions of them in an undignified manner. In India I see no difference between the manners of a king and a khidmutgar, indeed, I consider those of the latter superior."

Monday morning, March 10th, was spent with the American United Presbyterian Missionaries, and in a confirmation which they attended and expressed themselves pleased with. They had lately had an interview with the Maharajah in company with a native whom they had ordained under the name of the Rev. John Scott, and had presented His Highness with a copy of the Scriptures; he had met with a very ungracious reception. The Bishop remarks upon the practice of giving English or Yankee names to native Christians as *senseless and unpatriotic*, and of the habit of thrusting the Scriptures upon unwilling recipients; he says "I much doubt whether it was desirable to give him (the Maharajah) the Bible at all. They argue that even now perhaps some of his attendants may read it. It is equally, or even more, probable that they will light the fire with it; and this plan of thrusting the Word of God at unbelievers without any preparation certainly exposes it to contemptuous treatment, and it is likely to raise a prejudice against the donor and his religion."

On March 15th, the Bishop was at Amritsar midway between the rivers Beas and Ravee, owing its name which signifies the "Pool of Immortality" (Amrita, αμβροτος Saras) to the tank which Ram Das, the 4th great Sikh *Guru*, or spiritual guide, caused to be made here in 1581, and remarkable not only as being the religious capital of the Punjab, but also as being the first place where the Church of England established a mission to the Sikhs. The Bishop sums up his account of his visit to Ram Das's famous sanctuary, in the following words:—"The general effect of the whole exterior with its gilding glittering in the sun and its reflection in the clear waters of Immortality is extremely pretty; but from the small size of the temple and absence of grandeur and solemnity, I cannot give it a higher epithet. On the terrace round the temple sat groups of Sikhs listening to the chaunters of the Grunth venders of wooden combs to fasten up the unshorn locks of the faithful, of flowers for offerings to the temple, and others more or less interested or occupied about it. *The whole scene was cleaner, pleasanter, and gave a purer and better impression of worship, than those which we have witnessed at Kalighât, Benares and Hurdwar.*"

In connexion with the C.M.S. Mission School which he visited at Amritsar, the Bishop branches out into a comparison of the value of missionary school teaching, with that of itinerant preaching, which we give in his own words as we believe that it expresses an opinion which he never afterwards saw reason to change :—

"There is a tendency now certainly in the Committee of the Church Missionary Society at home and among some missionaries out here, to depreciate schools in comparison with preaching. Yet surely the great influence which a really kind, earnest, and able missionary must obtain over intelligent scholars, the undoubted improvement in the tone of morality, regard for truth, obedience and discipline effected in a well-ordered mission school (strongly asserted by the Peshawur missionaries), the favour which a good school wins for the mission as the source of great benefit to the city where it is planted (a fact resting on the evidence of the Agra Missionaries), and the general clearing away of ignorance, folly and superstition effected by education, are as likely to pave the way for Christ's spirit as the plan of hurrying from village to village, preaching for a day or two, and not re-appearing to deepen and confirm the impression of the visit till a year has passed away, and all that was said is forgotten. The Apostles brought with them two evidences of power and goodness; of the first by their miracles, of the latter by their lives. We should also bring forth, substituting for the miracles now withdrawn from the Church, the fact that knowledge, civilisation, activity, intellectual and material greatness, law, order, discipline, are all in the hands of Christian nations and in theirs only."

On the 23rd March 1860, the Bishop was at Kangra, opposite Dhurmsala. He mentions the view from the German missionary's house on this hill as an exceedingly grand one both towards the mountains and the plains. The former, he says, may be compared with Mont Blanc from the Flegère, the Jungfran from the Wengern Alp and the Orteler Spitz from the Stelvio. On the 24th March he was at Dhurmsala, 92 miles from Simla. At this point he alludes in his diary to a correspondence which he had had with Lord Canning in reference to the habitual disregard of Sunday which he had had occasion more than once to notice in the Viceregal progress. Lord Canning had defended himself by pleading that out of 22 Sundays he had only marched on seven. That a delay of more than one day in a place with his large escort led to difficulties in many cases about provisions, and consequent oppression to the natives. That his progress was a race against time. The Bishop seems still to have been of opinion that more regard might have been paid to the proper observance of the Lord's Day than had been, and it would be well, we think, if all Government officials in India, from the Viceroy downwards, paid a little more attention than they generally do to the principle for which the Bishop contended.

Before leaving Dhurmsala he paid a visit to 'Willy' Arnold's house for the purpose of being able to send his mother in England a full description of it. He also consecrated the Church and the burial ground "in which Willy's wife was laid." He notices in the Church a monument to their joint memory with the text "*There remaineth therefore a rest to the people of God,*" and remarks "the thought of rest is most appropriate to one of such untiring activity and incessant occupation as he. May he have found it in Christ Jesus!"

On March 26th, he descended from Dhurmsala 'through the rhododendrons' and in the early dawn of Sunday, April 1st, commenced the ascent of the hills towards Simla at Kalka, reaching Kussowlie, 20 miles short of Simla, before the morning was very far advanced. From Kussowlie, on April 4th, he went a distance of two miles, to the Lawrence Asylum at Sanawar. He confirmed eighty-one of the children and carefully examined the whole institution. In the Church he notices—at the west end a painted window to the memory of Lady Lawrence, and close to it a Gothic monument (a cenotaph of course, his body being interred at Lucknow) with the double inscription which he wished to be put upon his tomb, the text from Daniel "To the Lord, our God, belong mercies and forgivenesses," &c, and "Here lies Henry Lawrence who tried to do his duty."

He sums up his visit with the following remarks:—"Certainly this institution seems a wonderful place when I think what and where these soldiers' children might be without it. Either untaught, or at best only at Regimental schools, of which some are but poor affairs, living in barracks among many doubtful influences and losing health and vigour in the sultry plains; whereas now they are well cared for in body, soul and spirit, and (a rare privilege for shools of this character) they are brought under the direct influence of a conscientious clergyman instead of a trained school-master from Battersea."

The silence and stilness of Himalayas from the absence of those glacier streams which are so abundant in the Alps struck him much.

Easter-day, April 8th, found the Bishop at the Fort and Cantonment of Subathoo, the principal place of a small pergunnah, which passed under the power of the East India Company after the Goorkha war in 1815, which at present was dependent for its religious services upon the chaplain of Dugshai, eight miles away. And on Wednesday, 11th April, the final ascent from Siree, nine, miles up to Simla, was accomplished. The approach to it is described as through a forest of pines, evergreens and rhododendrons in full flower. 'Ravenswood, a house situate on a spur of the well-known Simla hill, Jack, was the Bishop's summer retreat.

Several ecclesiastical questions of considerable importance came before the Bishop during his 'industrious rest' at Simla in the summer of the year 1860. The first of these was the question of the employment of Government Churches at military stations for the Presbyterian services of Scotch regiments. The Bishop at once saw the reasonableness of such a course, with proper limitations and provisions for the maintenance of the Church of England's established rights over the buildings, and for the avoidance of unseemly quarrels and contentions in reference to the hours of service. In fact he had already, in 1859, on the application of a Punjab chaplain, given him authority to have the Scotch service held in his Church. Subsequently other cases of a similar kind began to crop up, and after a reference of the matter by the Governmeut to the Home Authorities it came before the Bishop for determination in correspondence with the Indian Government upon some general principle. Any kind of mixed service in which the English and Scotch chaplains might take a joint part, and which one or two of the chaplains seemed inclined by their example to favor, he forbade instantly and decidedly as irregular, and taking his stand upon the prior right of the Church of England to the buildings—(1) through episcopal consecration, (2) through the large funds spent upon them by members of the English Church in the way of private subscriptions or grants from the Diocesan Church Building Society in addition to the sums paid by Government, which he thankfully acknowledged, he succeeded in inducing Government to accept the principle expressed in the following extract from his last communication with the Governor-General upon the subject, and to frame an official notice accordingly :—

"I therefore earnestly hope that your Excellency maintaining the principle that these buildings are designed for the service of the Church of England, and placed under the care of the English Chaplain, acting under the authority of the Bishop, will simply direct that they shall be used, where it is possible, for the service of the Church of Scotland, particular cases being referred to the Bishop (whose consent in every case is necessary according to Dr. Lushington's opinion) who may fix the time for the English service, and therefore decide whether the hour of sunrise or sunset is available for the Scotch."

It was quite to be expected that this boon to the Scotch Establishment would induce applications in other quarters for a similar privilege, and it very soon did so in the Punjab where the influence of the American Presbyterians is so strong, chiefly it is to be feared through the absence of missionary zeal on the part of members of the Church of England in that quarter until recently. Officers in Her Majesty's service in many cases supported these applications, and did their utmost to get them favourably entertained at the Bishop's hands; but although he sympathized cordially with the spirit that called them forth, he had no hesitation whattever in giving them in every case a firm and decided negative. In fact, we may be sure that he saw that if the line were extended beyond the Scotch Establishment, where Government itself had drawn it, it must end in opening the Church doors promiscuously to all sects and parties whatever, who happened at any particular time and place to be numerous and strong. Of some officer who wrote to him upon the subject, and who seems to have improved the occasion by delivering himself at large upon the subject of 'new birth,' he said "I think Col. ——— most edifying on the campaign of Affghanistan, but singularly the reverse on Baptismal Regeneration."

To a chaplain who appears to have consulted him on the subject of meetings for discussion and reading of the Scriptures with members of other denominations, he wrote "I certainly do not envy you the Calvinism which your next subject suggests, for the older I grow and the more I read, the more I dislike that system not only from the untenable theory, but from its practical evils." Most wisely said Butler "though it were admitted that this opinion of necessity were speculatively true, yet with regard to practice it is as it were false. I have, however, no fear of your yielding the distinctive character of the English Church in your intercourse with your brethren of another, though I own one or two of the clergy seem to me to think that the way to stop the spread of dissent is to give up every point in which we differ from dissent. But you will not forget that the motto should be comprehension without compromise, and that conciliation and brotherly love are possible without the abandonment of principle. The calm and candid discussion of the meaning and application of Scripture between persons who agree in its divine authority is a clear gain."

Another chaplain seems to have consulted him about this time regarding the voluntary class-meetings of soldiers and their unauthorized administration to each other of the Holy Communion. The Bishop wrote in reply strongly reprobating the latter practice as unscriptural and schismatical, but recommended no interference with it except in the way of pastoral rebuke, brotherly remonstrance and the practical showing of a better way.

The well-known case of the Muzbee Sikhs was also brought to the Bishop's notice during this summer. These poor 'sweepers,' *out-castes*, who were descended from a band of Punjabee Thugs that had been broken up by the strong hand of Lord Dalhousie, had done excellent service as sappers and miners during the mutiny, and had got regularly incorporated into the native army. At the sack of Delhi some fragments of the Christian Scriptures had accidentally fallen into their hands, and a spirit of enquiry had arisen among them which some of their officers, assisted by various missionaries, had encouraged, and the result was an apparent tendency on the part of considerable bodies of them towards Christianity.

The lately quelled mutiny had done much to revive that traditionary feeling with the Indian Government that mission-work always brings with it the elements of danger to the State, so an order was issued cautioning officers against proselytising or in any open or official way encouraging the profession of Christianity among native troops. Some officer in reading the Government order seems to have added words of his own which led the troops to suppose that Government highly disapproved of their becoming Christians. The consequence was that the movement which had begun most hopefully, suddenly stopped, and the missionaries were deeply aggrieved and applied to the Bishop for redress. After considerable labour and correspondence it was made clear to all parties that the order of Government had been misinterpreted, and that so long as military discipline was preserved, they left the native soldier to chose his own religion, but still the tide not being taken at the flood, had lost its force, and the after-history of the regiments in which the religious awakening was manifested, seems to give credit to the assertion which the missionaries maintained, that the movement never recovered the check which the Government order gave to it, and that a golden opportunity was consequently lost of recovering a tribe as amenable to the influence of Christianity from the absence of caste as the Kohls or Sonthals. We will close our account of the Bishop's sojourn at simla with one or two allusions to his home correspondence at this period.

In a letter to the Rev. G. G. Bradley he says *sub finem* :— "It is most true that the present age has need of anxiety in its belief, but perhaps the extremity of the danger is the real security. Tennyson said to you what I have often thought and what I told poor Willy Arnold in almost our last interview, that the question was not so much of Christianity as of man's immortality. There seems to me no resting-place between Christianity and Positivism, and as to the latter I can only say, first, that Comte's religious system seems to me rather a subject for laughter than serious discussion, and next, that he bears unconscious testimony to the truths which he denies when he finds it necessary to provide such an extraordinary support for our religious feelings as his catechism. He testifies to the reality of those religious feelings and longings which, to my mind, point indubitably to a God; and given a God and immortality, and then I think that a Revelation is almost a necessary consequence."

Before leaving Simla, the Bishop paid a short visit to the station and cantonment of Kotgurh, (a little above 20 miles from Simla), and on his return wrote a careful report to Mr. Venn, Secretary of the C.M.S., upon the mission there, and generally upon the C.M.S. missions in the Punjab, recommending the strengthening and extension of them in some degree commensurate with the operations of other nonchurch bodies.

On the 1st October the Bishop left Simla and spent a toilsome month in visiting the stations lying to the south-east of it, such as Dehra, Mussoorie, Almorah and Nynee-Tal. On the 6th November he was at Bareilly, and on the 11th at Shahjehanpore, the scene of one of the most heart-rending massacres of 1857, which was consummated when the victims were assembled in St. Mary's Church for Divine Service on May 31st. Upon his course from this place to Benares which led him through Seetapoor, Lucknow, Roy Bareilly, Fyzabad, Gorruckpore, Jaunpore (famous for its noble monuments of the religious zeal of Jains, Buddhists, Hindus and Mahometans) we need not dwell. Interspersed with various ecclesiastical duties, and visits to every object of antiquarian or historic interest that came within reach, it gave the Bishop an opportunity of experiencing all the toils and pleasures of that camp-life which at this charming season of the Indian year, is so thoroughly enjoyable to any one who is blessed with health. The Bishop gives us an excellent idea of his *cortége* in the following muster which he puts down in his diary of 14th November "1 Prelate, 1 Prelate's wife, 1 Prelate's daughter, I Chaplain, 1 Docter, 1 Captain of Escort, 1 Nurse, 31

Servants, 4 Masalchies, 10 Bheesties, 8 Sweepers, 8 Sowars, 80 Sepoys, 31 Dooly Bearers, 1 Moonshee, 55 Kalassies, 10 elephants, 65 camels, 6 horses and ponies (besides those of the Sowars) 16 bullocks, 1 cow and her calf, goats, sheep, ducks, chickens, *ad libitum* (all but goats varying in number *de die in diem*, as they are devoured or successors bought), sundry Pariah dogs, 1 *cat, never seen but said to consume butter, sugar, tea and other provisions when they vanish unaccountably.*"

In February 1861, after an absence of 18 months, the Bishop's party were re-assembled in the Palace at Calcutta.

After a stay of six months in the Palace at Calcutta marked by the domestic incident of the departure of his faithful private chaplain, the Rev. T. Harris Burn, for England, through ill-health, and the historic one of the *Durbar* at Government House, at which Lord Canning received the thanks of the *Talookdars* of Oudh for the privileges which he had restored to them, the Bishop in the month of August departed for a two months' visitation of Assam.

The objects of interest on this north-eastern side of India, where the labour of man has hard work to contend with the abundant luxuriance of nature's fertility, were not at all to compare with those through which his previous tours had led him in the North-West, but still in the great Brahmaputra and in the thriving settlements which adjoin its mighty waters be found quite sufficient both of interest and occupation to compensate him for the toil he had to undergo. The heat during September appears to have been intense (the thermometer standing not unfrequently at 94°) without any proper means of mitigating it, so that he was frequently rendered perfectly prostrate through its effects. The tea-planters and Government officials, (in all cases where they were not laid up with Assam fever), received him cordially, and after penetrating as far as Tezpore he returned to Calcutta with a tolerably complete idea of the nature and requirements of this growingly important district of his diocese.

It was while he was *steaming* through the jungles of Assam, that news reached him of the famous *Nil Darpan* controversy, which in 1861 threw Calcutta and the whole of Bengal into such a tremendous ferment. The Bishop would not have been at all directly concerned in the matter, but the translator of the *Nil Darpan* which signifies '*Indigo-Mirror*,' and which was rather a low-lived native drama, lampooning the vices of the indigo-planters, happened to be the Rev. James Long, a missionary of the C.M.S.

It became his business, therefore, to make himself acquainted with all the facts of the case and to pass some kind of judgment upon the part which Mr. Long had borne in it. The preface to the translation contained an assertion that two of the Calcutta journalists were in the pay of the planters to support their interests, and treating this as a libel the Indian Landholders' Association had succeeded in getting the printer fined and the clergyman also mulcted Rs. 1,000 and imprisoned for one month. There being so far as he could judge nothing to prove that the clergyman had not acted in perfectly good faith, and with a sincere desire to benefit to too-long oppressed and enslaved Bengal indigo ryot, the Bishop considered the severe sentence amply sufficient and having explained to Mr. Long, in a communication of some length, the points in which he thought him to blame, he assured him that neither as Bishop nor as President of the Corresponding Committee of the C. M. S. had he any intention of moving further in the matter or attempting to add any ecclesiastical censures to the civil penalties already inflicted.

In a letter to a friend in England, dated Dibroghur in Upper Assam, September 3rd, 1861, the Bishop mentions having been recently "elected on the Syndicate or governing body of the Calcutta University," of which he continued ever afterwards one of the most active and influential members. The commencement of the cold weather found him again in Calcutta, busied about the Punjab Famine Relief Fund, a re-issue of the Prayer-book in Urdoo, and his Diocesan Hymn-book published about a year afterwards, and highly serviceable as a stepping-stone from 'Tate and Brady' to 'Hymns Ancient and Modern' which has now become almost universal throughout India.

Towards the end of November the Bishop started in the pilot brig *Mutlah* for his visitation of Burmah and the Straits. Early in the following month he was at Rangoon which evidently interested him much as one of the grand living centres of Buddhism.

After a visit to the great *Schwey Dagon* famous for its enormous altitude and as containing eight of *Gautamas* hairs, besides other memorials of preceding *Buddhas*, he writes:—"The Pagoda itself, as containing a relic, is the object of worship, and the prayers are in a manner addressed to Gotama: not that he can hear them or is conscious of the wants of his adorers, for he has attained *Nirwáná*, and is therefore in no intelligible sense existent, but by a law of nature the fact of worshipping him leads to births in happy conditions hereafter and ultimately to *Nirwáná*. Hence Buddhists may be said to adore Gotama's memory, and this is one of the numerous facts in which Buddhism is an anticipation of Comte's religion, and deprives that monstrous invention of even the merit of originality. In their atheism, their denial of a future state continuing through eternity, their adoration of the unconscious dead, the exclusively educational work of the priests, and the inexorable surpremacy of law, both systems are identical; they have also one good point in common—the unfailing certainty with which wrong leads the wrong-doer into suffering—though in this Gotama is superior to Comte, because by the doctrine of *Metempschychosis* he provides a manner in which punishment may follow crime, whereas I do not see how a wicked Comtist would practically be deterred from sin by any such belief, since in this life it is at least not visibly and obviously the case. Comte's devices of punishing a bad man's memory and dishonouring his carcase by exclusion from a consecrated grove surrounding the Temple of Humanity, are, of course, too ridiculous to be of any avail against the present pleasures of vice and self-indulgence. There is no doubt that the Buddhist doctrines are very superior to the Hindu, and that so far Gotama was a real reformer; but as I looked on one of his devotees praying to the unconscious and annihilated Buddha, I was, I trust, thankful for the revelation of a High Priest, who can be touched with the feeling of our infirmities and for the promise that he would be with us always, even unto the end of the world."

On the 6th December, the Bishop inspected and examined the American Baptist Mission Seminary for male and female Karen Christians conducted by Dr. and Mrs. Binney of Massachussetts at Kemendine, a suburb of Rangoon. He expresses himself as much encouraged by the sight of fifty Karen youths, all not only professing Christianity, but pledged to pastoral and missionary work among their countrymen, of whom some 30,000 were already baptised, and the practical moral which he drew was "that vigorous attempts should be directed to the conversion of all the *mountain tribes* of India, and every effort should be made to develop the native pastorate."

In his voyage up the Irrawaddy, which seems to have occupied about a fortnight, he was rather diverted when examining the famous Prome Pagoda, to find that the Kyoung, which Lord Dalhousie carried off thence, and which now stands 'as a trophy' in the Eden Gardens at Calcutta, had been replaced, at the cost of a rich Burmese, by a new one of costly construction on the exact spot whence the 'trophy' was taken, an evidence, he says that the feelings of the Buddhists had been outraged by the English Procousul's "silly and vain glorious" act of spoliation.

On Christmas-day he was at Moulmein, at the head of the lovely and picturesque Gulf of Martaban. Here he found an excellent S.P.G. Mission School containing 270 boys, of whom the great majority were Burmans with a few Chinese and Europeans or semi-Europeans. Their proficiency, which he rated as somewhat lower than a good school in Bengal, pleased him much, and he seems to have regarded the great taste, which the Burmese display for education, as a credit to their national school-masters the Poonghees (or Priests) who at least give the elements of learning with correctness, but launch out into every possible kind of absurdity when they attempt physical science. "The chief characteristic," he says, "of the system taught by Gotama's disciples is that they delight in the most inconceivable numbers, durations of time, and extensions of space, which transcend all human powers of memory and almost of imagination, but which are gravely set down in fiigures; while beings of twelve miles high are of quite ordinary occurrence, and some personages measure 800 miles from eyebrow to eyebrow, and 19,200 miles from the elbow to the tip of the finger."

On the 4th January 1862, the Bishop was at the Andamans, where he found no church and no regular clergyman. The latter defect he resolved to remedy as soon as possible after his return to Calcutta, and the appointment of a chaplain of Port Blair on his recommendation led, as was natural, in due time to the erection of the church.

On the 14th January, he was at Penang where the flags halfmast high first announced to him the death of the Prince Consort. On the 20th January he was at Malacca where he consecrated a new cemetery about a mile from the town and very near to the burial ground of the Chinese on which he makes the following remarks :—"Each grave occupied a space sufficient for six English graves; this practice being part of the general importance which the Chinese seem to attach to their funerals. Preparations for this event begin when their object is in the prime of health and vigour. As soon as a man has saved some money, his first object is to provide himself with a large, massive and handsome coffin, and this he commonly keeps in his verandah as long as he lives. I saw one of these strange pieces of furniture as we passed by Chinese houses. Often, too, a friend makes a present of a coffin to one to whom he desires to show his regard, nor is any gift considered a surer proof of affection and respect." He notices also the curious habit which the Chinese have of laying up the ashes of their ancestors and burning incense before them in the way of worship, having seen two tin vessels each containing handfuls of earth from the graves of the relations of the family, in a costly cabinet, at the house of a rich Chinese gentleman, to which he paid a visit.

Singapore, with its motley population of Chinese, Malays, Madrassees, Europeans, and 2,000 convicts from all parts of India and Ceylon, formed the *terminus* of the Bishop's voyage. Here he consecrated St. Anhrew's Church, a large and striking building, copied *mutatis mutandis* from Netley Abbey. He also administered confirmation to about 70 persons, and among them to some male and female Chinese; the males he says being attired in their full national dress with their long pigtails and other peculiarities, and the females in pink dresses, like great night shirts with wide embroidered trowsers and turned-up slippers!

The Bishop returned from his visitation with a conviction that Burmah and the Straits should as soon as possible be cast off from the see of Calcutta and taken up on their own ground, as none but a Mithridates or a Mezzofanti could be episcopally efficient in Bengali, Hindustani, Burmese, Malay, Chinese and Tamil.

By the 24th February the Bishop was again in Calcutta, and writes in his diary—"Thank God for all His mercies through Jesus Christ. We return indeed with sad remembrances of the mournful events, public and private, which have marked the tour, and especially of one *who went out with us but has not come back again.*" The allusion here is to the Rev. J. Rofe, his temporary domestic chaplain, who had died on the voyage. The public events, alluded to, are the death of Lady Canning and of the Prince Consort. Early in March the Bishop consecrated the small cemetery in the Government House gardens at Barrackpore, where Lady Canning had been buried under her favourite tree. On the 18th March, soon after the arrival of the new Governor-General, Lord Elgin, Lord Canning sailed for England, and the Bishop was among the party who were assembled to give him a final shake of the hand and to bid him farewell.

The hot weather of 1862 from April to November was spent by the Bishop and his family at Darjeeling, or, as it should more properly be written and pronounced, Dorjêling. He gives in his journal the following derivation of the name:—"I find that Darjeeling clearly means place of holiness," for *dorje* is * * the sceptre borne by a Lama, the sceptre of the priesthood; and that this is its special sense in reference to Darjeeling, and not either a regal sceptre, or lightning (which it also means, the sceptre being like forked lightning) seems proved by the existence of the ruined Lamaserai on the top of Darjeeling hill." He found a source of much refreshment and of never-ceasing delight, whenever the weather was propitious, in the noble amphitheatre of the Sikkim Himalayahs under which Darjeeling lies, and especially of Kunchinjinga the second highest mountain in the world, about forty miles north of it. Kunchinjinga, he says, is in the Thibetan language 'covered with eternal snow.' Kon = being = snow, chin = covered, and jing = coequal or coeval. The frequent, however, and in some months almost incessant, downpour of rain he found very depressing, and it rendered expeditions among the mountains very rare, and at most times altogether impossible.

But at various intervals he found opportunity to visit Hope-Town, a tea settlement at a somewhat lower level than Darjeeling, and situate among the hills about ten miles to the west of it, and also to manage an expedition, twelve miles eastward, to the Rungeet river; "in the course of which," he says, "we passed through a succession of varied beauties with grand views of Kunchinjinga and of the snowless but prominent peak of Tendong, the Ararat of these parts, *for on it, according to the Sikkim legend, a boat containing human beings rested after the flood."* The barracks also on Mount Senchal and the conical hill above them so famous for its unrivalled view of the snowy range, and of Mount Everest (in Nepal) the highest mountain in the world, came in for more than one visit.

He took upon himself the superintendence of a soldiers' Bible class at Jellapahar which involved a journey of a mile or two to the westward and back again, week by week. He complains in reference to this that he found himself unable to draw the men into conversation, and regrets that all the talking was on his side. The men, however, thoroughly appreciated the Bishop's familiar expositions, and often alluded to them afterwards with feelings of gratitude. In the matter of correspondence, the first subject which he took up was that of the missions of the S. P. G., and he indited a long and careful letter to the Home Secretary, saying that as the C. M. S. was working so well in the North-West, and the S. P. G. had broken ground already with some success in Assam and Burmah and the Straits, he considered it might be a good plan that, without at all interfering with stations already set on foot, the two Societies should agree to divide the Diocese of Calcutta between them on the general plan that the C. M. S. should take the North-West, and the S. P. G. the East and North-East. It is only want of funds that has prevented the S. P. G. from giving fuller effect to the Bishop's plan, and they have within the last few years somewhat extended and strengthened their missions in Burmah, where, in consequence of the friendly attitude of the king, their operations at the capital city of Mandalay have been considerably amplified.

The Bishop next entered into a long correspondence with the Committee of the additional Clergy Society with a view to inducing them to relax their rules somewhat, so as to increase the number of their clergy and supply the spiritual wants of the numerous small communities who, scattered here and there throughout the land, were, to use Bishop Middleton's expressive phrase, "virtually excommunicated." The caution of the Committee who were, in a certain sense, very properly afraid of running into danger and debt, by changing their rules and increasing their liabilities, evidently tried the Bishop's patience. At last, however, he seems to have obtained the acknowledgment of the principle that the Society should go hand-in-hand with Government in supplying the spiritual wants of stations, whether mainly occupied by Government servants or not; and also the boon of a grant towards the *inevitable* parsonage-house which the station was called upon to supply. The result of the change in the Society's *modus operandi* was a rise in the number of its *employés* in four years from eight to twenty; but its increased liabilities have scarcely been followed by adequate public subscriptions and support, and the most careful vigilance has been necessary on the part of its managers to avoid prospective insolvency. We close our account of the sojourn at Darjeeling with an extract or two from the Bishop's journal and correspondence, illustrative of the religious habits of the Thibetans and Lepchas.

In October he writes:—"Among the events of these last days I must not omit a visit from the Tchibu Lamma, a Buddhist priest of high rank, Vakeel to the Rajah of Sikkim, and a just friend to the English, from whom he has received a large grant of land on Simonbong, a hill between Tongloo and the valley of the little Runjeet. He was attired in red with a yellow cap, and as he approached the fern-collector prostrated himself flat on the earth. The Lama talked very bad Hindustani and so did we, so that I could not get out of him as much Buddhist theology as I could wish, especially as to the position which the Delai Lama at Lassa occupies in the system, and how he fits it with Sakya Muni of old and the next incarnation of Buddha, who is expected hereafter. He told us, however, intelligibly, how a new Delai Lama is chosen or rather revealed to the Thibetans. When the Delai Lama dies, the people wait eagerly till some child in Thibet of five years old announces himself as his successor. As soon as he does so, articles of furniture and dress are brought to the child, and he is asked to select those which belonged to his predecessor, *i. e.*, to himself, since he is only the new manifestation or incarnation of his predecessor. Then a number of servants are submitted to his inspection, and he points out those who attended on him in his former existence. 'This is my khansamah;' 'this is my bearer,' he says, and so on as Tchibu explained to us going through the various Hindustani names for servants. If he passes correctly, these two tests of the property and the servants his claims to the spiritual sovereignty are admitted, and he is duly installed and worshipped at Lassa."

In a letter to Rev. J. N. Simpkinson, dated Darjeeling 1862, he gives the following account of the Lepchas:—"Our chief human beings are Lepchas, said to be the aborigines of these mountains: fair in complexion, wholly beardless, with long hair twisted in tails down their backs, so that it is hard to distinguish men and women, Buddhists after a sort, filthily dirty, not dainty in their food, inasmuch as they eat cats and snakes, and *performing their devotions by the singular process of twisting round and round small brass cylinders on a wooden handle."*

In November 1862 the Bishop left Darjeeling, and having been rejoined by his Domestic Chaplain, the Rev. T. H. Burn who had just returned from furlough in England, proceeded upon a visitation tour through Central India. An idea of his course and of his rate of progress may be obtained from the dates which we find in his journal:—*Benares*, 30th November 1862; *Maihor* (between Allahabad and Jubbulpore), 9th December; *Jubbulpore*, 11th December; *Seoni*, 18th December; *Residency, Seetabuldi, Nagpore*, Christmas Day 1862; *Hoshungabad*, 31st December; *Panibijwara*, 4th January, 1863; *Mhow*, Epiphany, 1863; *Sehore*, 16th January; *Saugor*, 22nd January; *Lullutpore*, N. W. P., 28th January; *Jhansi*, 2nd February; *Cawnpore*, 11th February.

The travelling arrangements in the Central Provinces were far inferior in those days to what they are now, and the perils and hardships which the Bishop encountered in mountain-pass, jungle and wilderness, from bad roads, bad dooly bearers, want of shelter and occasionally want of food, were quite apostolic. On one occasion a whole village turned out at night with lighted torches to guard the Bishop's party through a mountain-pass which was infested by a man-eating tiger; but happily on this as well as on other occasions when similar dangers were threatened, the wild beasts of the forest kept out of the way, and although his chaplain suffered somewhat from the toils of the journey the Bishop and his attendant doctor came through unscathed.

At Nagpore the Bishop inaugurated a new school for Europeans and Eurasians on the plan of his scheme for schools in the hills and plains, of which we shall give some account hereafter. This school, when we passed through Nagpore in December 1869, was flourishing and doing useful work.

He paid a visit to the Rajah of Nagpore ('representative of the dethroned Bhoonsla dynasty') whose palace, he says, is remarkable as a fine specimen of Mahratta architecture, consisting of long colonnades and arcades of carved wood, each pillar being the trunk of a teak tree with projecting caves, oriel windows and flat roofs, the general effect being very massive and sombre. Of the Rajah himself, he writes as follows:—" He is of a low *caste*—a *Sudra;* but he had a crowd of frowsy objects in attendance, whom he called *hamara Brahmanlog* ('my Brahmins') and whom Temple treated with little deference. Certainly if these tykes really keep the Rajah in complete order, force him to maintain them, impose penances and fines, and mix themselves up with his whole life and death, it is an instance of the triumph of the spiritual over the secular, scarcely reached by Gregory the VII, or Becket. For there he stood blazing with gold and jewels, with gold and silver maces round him, with attendants fanning him and with the Chief Commissioner (Sir Richard Temple), and the Bishop treating him with great civility on a raised platform. Two or three steps below were these Brahmins dirty, mean-looking, some in their dotage, in coarse white garments and bare legs, no better in appearance than the coolies who had borne our palanquins. Yet they appear to be quite necessary to him and to exercise over him a complete spiritual despotism. This scene took place in the temple of Krishna in his garden, of which they were the ministers and guardians."

On New Year's eve 1862-63, he writes at *Hoshungabad:*— "The sorrows that have most troubled me are the public deaths, which India has this year had to mourn and the undeniable growth of the difficulties connected with Scripture and Church questions, which continue without any opposition, or solution, or attempt at rectification with which I can thoroughly sympathize. *A true Christian prophet is surely needed.* May God raise up among us those who are fitted to strengthen the bulwarks of His Church!"

Of Mhow, he says:—"Mhow is an ugly place, perhaps the ugliest cantonment I ever saw. It is quite as brown and burnt as Allahabad or Cawnpore. It is almost wholly treeless. Very few of the houses have compounds, but are stuck promiscuously and on no plan or system about the arid and rocky plain. There is only one relief to the view as almost every where in Central India. There are distant hills; but these are mere treeless rocks!"

At Saugor, he writes:—"To-day the fort has been visited which rises above the lake and commands the city. There is a fine extent of wall with picturesque round towers, but the walls are said to be weak and incapable of standing a siege. Here, in 1857-58, all the residents of Saugor, three hundred in number, including the present chaplain and his family, were shut up for six months for fear of the Gwalior Contingent, till they were relieved by Sir Hugh Rose."

At Jhansi he consecrated the cemetery and memorial building erected over the remains of 66 persons murdered there in 1857. He expresses infinite regret that the building was such 'a mixture of Paganism, Mahometanism and ugliness."

Arrived at last at Cawnpore, he notices with great delight and surprise the wonderful transformation which had passed over the place since his first visit to it, describing it "as a change from a waste howling wilderness to an attractive and pretty station." His chief object there at present was the consecration of the precincts of the Fatal Well and of the adjoining cemeteries. The Viceroy (Lord Elgin) and the Vicereine with all their attendants, Sir Hugh Rose and his Staff, Chief Commissioner Wingfield and his Staff from Oudh, all the chief authorities from Lucknow, Allahabad, Futtehpore, the Archdeacon and nine other clergy, and some thousand soldiers were present. The ceremonial consisted of the service usual on such occasions, its chief feature being the address from the Bishop which he had previously carefully prepared, and which spoken from the heart upon such a sacred and soul-stirring spot watered with the blood of so many martyrs to the Christian faith, produced a profound and lasting impression upon all who heard it.

The next date in the Bishop's Journal is Agra, February 18th. A question of vital importance in the education and material well-being of India had lately come on the *tapis* here. A Christian boy of the sweeper caste, who had displayed considerable natural ability, had been admitted by the Principal of St. John's College (C. M. S.) among the high-caste Brahmin students, with a view to his instruction in the higher branches of learning, for which he seemed so well qualified. The pride of the parents of the high-castes was affronted, and unless the obnoxious sweeper boy was sent a-packing they declared that they would very soon empty the school. The Principal, however, stood firm, and the result was that the numbers were reduced in a few days from upwards of 200 to about 20.

The Bishop arrived just at the critical time when Christian wisdom with a handful was battling in an apparently unequal contest with suicidal birth-pride backed by thousands, and he at once threw all his weight into the Christian scale. Being called upon to preside on the annual prize-day, when a large concourse of natives were present, he went thoroughly in his presidential speech into the whole question, and showed most convincingly how the greatness of England had arisen from her recognizing taleut in any of her children, whether high or low born, and rewarding it by promotion to the highest post and places; aud he predicted for India decadence and disgrace if she persevered in caste-prejudices; honour, and advancement, if she shook herself free from them and took up the principle of the universal brotherhood of all ranks and classes in Christ, and the right of every man, however, born to find in society the rank and office for which Providence by natural endowment had prepared him. The effect of the Principal's firmness backed by the Bishop's weighty words soon produced its effect. Certain of the bigoted malcontents erected a rival institution, and by a strange misnomer instituted it the *Victoria* College, but victory was palpably on the other side, for in a few weeks the St. John's College had fully regained its previous complement, and was even more prosperous than it had been before the secession.

This was the only great public occasion on which the caste-question came prominently before Bishop Cotton, and he showed by his conduct in regard to it, what he also repeatedly declared in his second charge, aud on other occasions, that he fully concurred in the decision which Bishop Wilson had given as to the *inadmissibility of caste in any shape into the Christian system.* "*A decision*" *he said, which he trusted,* "*would not be reversed or meddled with by any of his successors, and certainly never by himself.*"

After his return to Calcutta the Bishop entered into a lengthy correspondence with Government in reference to the ecclesiastical wants of the Central Provinces and the anomalous state of the boundary question between the Dioceses of Calcutta, Madras and Bombay. Suggesting that Mhow and Indore belonged geographically to Bombay, and that the fact of Kamptee and Seetabuldee having been served so long by Madras chaplains, rendered their transfer to the See of Calcutta, on the annexation of the Central Provinces to Bengal, most inconvenient, unless the staff of Bengal Chaplains was enlarged. No rectification, however, of the Diocesan frontiers has yet been attempted by Government, nor has the number of the Bengal chaplains been increased, and anomalies and inconveniences (such as the Bishop complained of) are likely to continue until either Burmah or the Punjab is erected into a separate see.

The summer of 1863 from April to the commencement of November was spent by the Bishop at the Palace, Calcutta. His correspondence during this period as given in his biography, is unusually scanty, nor are we favoured with any extracts from his diary, so that we may suppose that apart from the usual quiet routine of ecclesiastical duty his time was chiefly occupied in the composition of his second triennial charge. The visitation commenced on Tuesday, 3rd November, with full morning service with a sermon by the Rev. H. Burney (Chaplain of Hazareebaugh), followed by administration of the Holy Communion; and the charge, which occupied nearly four hours in delivery, was given after the Litany on Wednesday, 4th November. It commenced with some encouraging particulars regarding mission work in Tinnevelly, Chota Nagpore, Burmah, Umritsur, &c. The Bishop then gave his ideas of proper Christian work among soldiers, drawing an admirable picture of a model military station-work among Eurasians and among natives. He then gave some particulars of progress during the last three years, stating that there had been—

Churches, consecrated...	...	...	23
Priests, ordained	...	... ...	22
Deacons, do.	...	... ...	24
Native Priests and Deacons, ordained		...	5
Confirmees	...	... ...	1,085

He also mentioned that the ordained clergy under S. P. G. had risen from 16 to 24 in number, and under C.M.S. from 44 to 50.

He then passed to matters generally concerning the Church of England at large, and after alluding to the difficulty which the Bishops at home so much lamented in obtaining duly qualified ordinees, witnessed by the fact that, whereas in 1852, the ordinees were 614 in number, in 1862 they were only 570, he discussed the question of the advisability or non-advisability of Liturgical Revision as a means of allaying the doubts and dissensions which unhappily prevailed. Looking upon the Common Prayer-book as a sacred trust, never lightly to be altered or tampered with, he still maintained that there were some points in it which might advantageously be subjected to revision as time went on, but those points he contended were at the present period but few. A rubric here and there, a remodelling of the calendar, and a second form of burial for non-communicants were all that he would give his sanction to. For the substance of the Athanasian Creed, he stoutly contended as a most valuable heirloom to the church, and especially so among the subtle and speculative natives of India.

The Bishop's remarks upon these points produced a marked impression upon all who heard them; but we think that the concluding portion of the charge, which treats of the inspiration of Holy Scripture, is that which must always impart to it its most important and lasting value. The Bishop begins by saying—"Let me express my regret that we are compelled to treat it (that is, the inspiration and historical trust of Holy Scripture) as a matter for argument and intellectual discussion at all, instead of receiving the blessed gift of God's written word, in the simple spirit of humble thankfulness as the means of our growth in self-knowledge and Christian holiness. Many who have watched the power of Scripture to comfort the mourner and cheer the dying with the hope of immortality must loath the dry husks of critical discussion, and turn with repugnance from theories of inspiration, while still refreshed by the pure streams with which the Prophets and Evangelists have watered the Church of Christ." The Bishop then examines and rejects the two opposite theories of inspiration, the first which represents every word and syllable of the Bible as actually dictated by the Holy Ghost, just as if High Heaven were open, and we heard God speaking to us with human voice, and the other which sees no difference between the inspiration of the writers of Scripture, and that of other great men, who by their piety or genius have moved the world."

We have not space to follow out in detail the able and masterly way in which both these theories are refuted, but must content ourselves with simply quoting one sentence which seems in few words to embrace the Bishop's own views on the subject. "The first result, then, of a candid enquiry into the character of Scripture, must be the recognition of the Divine and human elements which are combined in its composition. It is emphatically God's book; but God employed human agents to write it, and did not supersede their individuality, their tastes, their intellectual gifts, their natural dispositions, their powers of observation. In its transmission to us it has been subject to human revision, but God has providentially watched over it, so that we find in it a perfect declaration of His Will and a sure foundation for our faith. *But if you ask me for a precise theory of inspiration, I confess that I can only urge you to repudiate all theories; to apply to theology the maxim which guided Newton in philosophy* "Hypotheses non fingo," *and to rest your teaching upon the facts which God has made known to us.*"

A few days after the delivery of his charge, the Bishop went on board the P. and O. steamer *Nemesis* with a view to commencing his quinquennial visitation as Metropolitan of the dioceses of Madras, Bombay and Ceylon. After spending a week at Madras, where, in addition to a round of constant and varied occupation, he succeeded in getting up a public meeting to forward the Duff memorial scheme, he left, in company with Bishop Gell, whom he had persuaded to accompany him to Bombay, for Beypore on the western coast, and both prelates embarked without delay in the Government steamer *Dalhousie* which was in waiting.

Two halts were made on the voyage—The first at Honore from which place an excursion was made to the famous Gerseppa Falls, the other at Goa. We have an account of the Bishop's impressions, of the picturesque, but now plague-striken and desolate old city of Goa in a letter to Dean Stanley, dated six weeks later. After describing the ruined state of the Convents, Abbeys, Inquisition buildings, and the Viceregal Palace, he says, the three churches which still remain (the Cathedral, St. Cajetan, and the Church of Bom Jesus) that the last is the most interesting as containing Xavier's tomb. "The shrine," he writes, "is adorned by four fine *bas reliefs* in bronze, representing Xavier's preaching, baptizing, persecution and dying; and on the top of the shrine, which is very lofty, rests the coffin of solid silver containing his body. Just outside the chapel is a portrait of him, said to be perfectly authentic and representing a face of marvellous pathos and devotion. I confess, however, that while he deserves the title of the Apostle of India for his energy, self-sacrifice and piety, I consider his whole method thoroughly wrong, its results in India and Ceylon most deplorable, and that the aspect of the native Christians at Goa and elsewhere shows that Romanism has had a fair trial at the conversion of India and has entirely failed. Let us only hope and pray that Protestantism may do better. The one bright example of a flourishing and industrious settlement of native Romanists is at Bettia near Nepaul, and with it neither Xavier nor the priests of Goa had anything to do."

On the 30th November 1863, the Bishop arrived in Bombay. The fortnight which he spent here was occupied in assisting at the Advent services at the Cathedral and the Church at Colaba; in inspecting and examining the various educational institutions, male and female, for which Bombay is so famous; in episcopal conferences with his brethren, Bishops Gell and Harding; in long and interesting conversations with the Free Kirk Missionary, Dr. Wilson (the Dr. Duff of Bombay); and in excursions to the Caves of Elephanta and the Parsee Towers of Silence on Malabar Hill; the Buddhist Caves at Karli, &c., &c.

The Church at Colaba built as a memorial to those who fell in the Affghan war, and designed by Henry Conybeare, he justly praises as one of the finest in India.

The Dakhma Tomb, or Temple of Silence, which he visited, he compares in appearance to one of the circular buildings which mark the openings into the Kilsby Tunnel of the North-Western Railway. Their diameter, however, is far larger. Their interior was described to the Bishop by the Parsee priest in charge "as a sloping shelf (resembling a huge wheel with a central well) divided into three compartments, the upper one for men, the middle for women, the lower for children, and when a corpse is brought for burial, it is placed in its proper compartment, and left there to be devoured by the hideous vultures which are always in waiting on the top of the tower. The bones, from time to time, are swept into the bottom of the well by a priest, and there are drains to carry off the water. If a Parsee dies at a distance from a Dakhma, his body is exposed on the top of the highest hill in the neighbourhood."

Shiva's rock-cut Cave-temple at Elephanta has been so often described by others that we need not dwell on the Bishop's account of it.

The Buddhist Cave at Karli, just above the Bhore Ghaut, on the road by rail to Poona, the Bishop visited in company with Dr. Wilson. He says it is one of the most striking of Indian sights and really magnificent. Passing the richly carved entrance, you find yourself "in a vast excavation resembling the choir of a great Gothic cathedral, divided into three aisles by two rows of columns, with fantastic capitals composed of elephants and their riders ending in a semi-circular apse which is filled up (as the east end of a Christian church is by its altar) by a *daghoba*, a bell-shaped structure, covering a relic of Buddha or one of his saints." Above the cave is a *vihara* or monastery, also cut out of the rock, and a *choultry* or hospice for pilgrims. "The whole," the Bishop says, "is attributed to the time of Asoka, the great patron of Buddhism, about 200 B.C."

One remarkable feature in the Bishop's doings at Bombay was an address which he delivered to 300 native young men, Hindus and Parsees, collected by Mr. James Wilson of the C. M. S. Mission. While showing in eloquent and forcible terms the superior claims to Christianity to those of either Buddhism or Brahmanism or Mahometanism, he protested against the confusion between "progress" and mere go-a-headism, and said that *unless intellectual progress was accompanied by moral and spiritual progress, it involved a good deal of retrogression*—a statement which he illustrated by a sketch of 'Young Bengal,' and by some of the facts already produced in his charge.

On the 14th December the Bishop left Bombay for Ceylon.

The Bishop devoted eighteen days to his visitation of Ceylon, spending Christmas-day with Bishop Claughton at Colombo, and New Year's-day at Kandy. At Kandy he paid a visit to the temple of the *Dalada* (which he identifies with the Latin *Dens* and the Greek ὀδούς) so called because it contains a precious relic, in the shape of a long piece of discoloured ivory, unquestionably part of an elephant's tusk, which has been dignified with the name of Sakya's tooth. He was not allowed to see the relic itself, the keeper of the key having conveniently absconded for the occasion, but he gives the following account of its surroundings. "The tooth is guarded by a large iron cage (secured by many locks) within which is a silver gilt shrine, in the *Daghoba* (the tope of Bhilsa, the Pagoda of Burmah) richly adorned with jewels, and doubtless both pretty and gorgeous. Candles burnt before it and about it ; the smell of the flowers was exactly like the odour of incense and the resemblance of the whole to the chapel and shrine enclosing a Roman Catholic relic was most striking. In another chapel hard by are some costly images of Buddha, of rock crystal; and at no great distance is a colossal image of him, thirty-six feet long lying down, with his head resting on his hand supposed to be in the act of receiving *nirvána* or annihilation."

About the beginning of the second week in January 1864, the Bishop crossed the Gulf of Manaar in the Governor of Ceylon's official steamer Yacht, and landing at Tuticorin commenced his tour through the Tinnevelly Missions with Dr. Caldwell for his guide. On January 10th, he was at Palamcottah; on the 11th, at Tinnevelly; on the 16th, at Megnanapuram (town of true wisdom;) on the 18th, at Suviseshapuram (*Gospel town*); on the 19th, at Dr. Caldwell's own station Edyen Koody (abode of the shepherd), so called through an unconscious prophecy by the heathen themselves; on the 22nd he arrived at Nagercoil, a suburb of the town of Kotan and the head-quarters of the London Missionary Society in Travancore. The tour through our Tinnevelly Church Missions, therefore, must have occupied him about ten days. He mentions the church at Megnanapuram as a building of very considerable beauty, in correct early English, * * * the finest church that he had seen in the presidency and one of the finest in any of the three presidencies. At Edyen Koody, he says, "one of the most successful operations is lace-making, which Mrs. Caldwell has imported from Buckinghamshire, and which women carry on in the verandah of the parsonage. This lace is so much sought throughout India, that the profits of each woman average eight rupees a month, of which four rupees are for herself and four for the Mission."

The Bishop was deeply impressed with the reality of the work which Christianity had done among the Shánárs (Palmyra-climbers) of Tinnevelly. And after noticing in a letter to the Rev. G. G. Bradley the cordiality existing between the labourers under our two great Missionary Societies, S. P. G. and C. M. S., the mapping out of the country into parochial districts, each with church parsonage and schools, and (England's great want) *small prayer-houses in the minor hamlets*, the progress of education, the increase of industry, order, cleanliness, domestic purity, improvement in worldly circumstances, the efforts made for the eradication of the great national Indian vice of prevarication and untruthfulness, he concludes altogether, I do not think that any one can go through the Tinnevelly missions without being the better for it, and I feel that my own faith in the Gospel has been strengthened by the journey and by the actual sight of what Christianity can do. "I have heard of Thee by the hearing of the ear, but now mine eye seeth Thee."

At Nagercoil the Bishop was the guest of Mr. Duthie, one of the missionaries of the London Society, and '*with all due terror of the Guardian*' he records that sitting between two Nonconformist ministers he passed two selected classes of their native converts through a tolerably searching examination in the rudiments of Christian Theology; and that the answers were remarkably good, specially those given by the women; 'a strking contrast,' he observes, 'to the condition of the female sex before Christianity spread its influence over the land.'

From the London Society's Missions the Bishop passed on to the north-west, travelling for a considerable distance in a narrow row boat by the strips of inland sea which line the coast in this quarter; and on the 25th January he was at Cottyam, the head-quarter of the Church Missions of Travancore, and also one of the centres of the Syrian Church. The only new feature in church affairs there which he notices, is that there had been an attempt made on the part of the priests of the Syrian Church and the missionaries of the C. M. S. to work together in the management of a training College; but the attempt, as was *natural*, had failed, and the two parties now found they could be much better friends if they each went on in their own way.

The Metran Athanasius was unfortunately absent during the period of the Bishop's visit, but the *Cathanars* (priests of the Syrian Church) received him cordially and asked him to address their congregation which he did through an interpreter. He concludes his account of his visit as follows:—"The neighbourhood of the Christian Church is plainly improving the Syrians; and the present Metran Athanasius, who was not at Cottyam during our visit, is a reformer. He does not hinder his people, nor even his deacons, from pursuing their studies in our college; he has encouraged the *Cathanars* to give the cup to the laity, the practice having generally been to give the wafer dipped in the wine; he has ordered them to say the prayers, as far as possible, in the Malayalim, and even to preach, though they have a difficulty in obeying this order as none of them have been trained or accustomed to do so. Unhappily he does not seem to carry much weight personally. Nor is there much to be hoped from Antioch where the church is sunk in superstitious bigotry, and whence a prelate, named Curilos, has lately been sent to check and watch the reforming tendencies of Athanasius.

On his way back to Madras from the western coast, the Bishop spent ten days in the Nilgherries at Ootacamund, from whence he writes to various English relatives and friends, reviewing his recent tour and dilating upon the various beauties and curiosities of the *Blue Mountains* in such terms as the following:—"As to races and religions we have seen Parsees at Bombay worshipping the setting sun, and exposing their dead on high towers to vultures; we have recalled the past greatness of Buddhism in the magnificent cave at Karli, and witnessed its present apathy and degeneracy in the priests and worshippers of Kandy, who gather round the temple where Buddha's tooth is enshrined; we have visited Syrians at Kottyam, anathematising Nestorius and the council of Chalcedon and repeating the Nicene Creed without the words acknowledging the double procession; white Jews at Cochin, some with blue eyes and light hair boasting of the perfect purity of their Hebrew blood, like St. Paul to the Philippians, but without the accompanying confession 'that what things were given him these he counted loss for Christ;' black Jews in the same place, probably either Hindu converts to Judaism, or illegitimate descendants of the white Jews, not, as some have vainly imagined, fugitives from Pharoah Necho, or I know not what other Egyptian king; castes and races on the west coast, including two royal families, in which, owing to the horrid custom of polyandry, the inheritance and even the Rajahship passes to the sister's son as the only one certainly inheriting the family blood; and, lastly a mountain race in these hills called the Todas, exacting tribute, as lords of the soil, from certain Hindu folk who fled up here from the persecutions of the Mahomedans, and worshipping in a manner which would gratify the Comtists as a purely *industrial* form of religion since it consists entirely *in churning butter*." By the middle of March 1864 the Bishop had returned to Calcutta.

We may commence our chronicle of the events of the hot weather of 1864, which was spent by the Bishop in the palace at Calcutta, by alluding to two important letters written at the commencement of this period.

One of these was addressed to the Rev. F. Farrar, the present master of Marlborough School, who had used the expression in a recent communication with him—"*We are upon the eve of a new Reformation.*" The Bishop professes himself unable to understand the expression, and fears that it does not mean growth in knowledge, piety, wisdom, and good works, but a general belief in the current Biblical speculations of the day, having as its apostles Renan and others of our own land, in which sense he cannot allow that it has any right to be called a '*Reformation*' at all, but rather a denial of a supernatural revelation altogether—a reduction of our Lord to the level of Plato, Buddha, and Mahomet, and a total upsetting of the foundations of the Christian faith.

In reference to another expression in Mr. Farrar's letter 'that he can *disprove from Scripture* the fact of our common descent from Adam and Eve,' the Bishop says that if Mr. Farrar can really do what he asserts every body may be very much obliged to him if such a view be really the true one; but he expresses the strongest objection to the practice of Colenso, Wilson and others of that school, absolutely ignoring and vilipending the authority of our Lord and His Apostles, or the express statements of other parts of Scripture for the sake of some baseless or half-formed conjecture, or some alleged scientific discovery imperfectly ascertained, and of which the full bearings are not known.

The other letter is to the most Reverend Mar Athanasius, Bishop and Metran, in reply to one from the Metran to signify his regret at his absence during the Metropolitan's visit. Expressing his deep interest in the venerable Syrian

Church of Travancore, the Bishop recommends as the best steps to primitive importance and purity—1, a faithful discharge of ministerial duties combined with a blameless life, 2, circulation of the Holy Scripture; 3, sound learning and religious education; 4, preaching and ministering in the vernacular.

One of the Bishop's first acts after his return was to call upon the new Viceroy, Sir John Lawrence. Not many days afterwards he assisted at the ceremony of the Laying of the Foundation Stone of the new Sailors' Home by the Viceroy, drawing up a short form of prayers for the occasion. This admirable institution had previously been located in a position most unfavourable for the welfare of the sailors, at the bottom of Bow Bazaar, in the very centre of all the worst grogshops of the city.

The foundation of the Missionary Pastorate—the least successful perhaps of all the schemes which Bishop Cotton initiated—belongs to the summer of 1864. Its object was to provide for the benefit of the lowest class of Eurasians in the streets and lanes of Calcutta—a class which, though nominally Christian, exhibits a lamentably small amount of the Christian virtues; the services of an ordained minister who should make it his especial province to go in and out among them, and reclaim them to something like decency of conduct and life. The means for the pastor's maintenance were provided partly out of funds, at the Bishop's and Archdeacon's disposal, partly from grants from the various church vestries, and partly by a small Government grant-in-aid. The first missionary pastor, himself an Eurasian, specially ordained to the office, carried on the work for upwards of a year, and was then succeeded by a second who continued it for a few years longer; but whether it were from the want of a more definite field than the whole of a large city to work upon, or whether it were from the absence of cordial co-operation between the regular chaplains and the pastor, who seemed to be going about with a sort of roving commission from the Bishop, or whether it were from the difficulty which the various vestries found in providing their *quotas* of subscription; the result was that before the year 1870 the scheme died a natural death, and the office was abolished.

A more auspicious event for the Eurasians of the better class was the consecration in the summer of 1864 of the new Church of St. James, which mainly, through the exertions of Archdeacon Pratt, had again sprung to life in a much fairer form than it originally wore, on the eastern edge of the Circular Road, at some distance from its former site. A parsonage house for the chaplain was also procured. The St. James's School already existed on the spot. The Boswell Hall (so called in memory of a former chaplain—the Rev. Robert Bruce Boswell) was built through the exertions of the chaplain in charge, and by these means the district of St. James's was enabled to exhibit the most perfect sample of the Parochial system which is to be found in Calcutta.

Such were some of the works for the benefit of Europeans and Eurasians with which the Bishop was connected during the course of this summer. As to the natives and the native church we may mention here, that as he always exhibited a lively and practical interest in the University of Calcutta, and on every possible occasion was present at, and took part in, the deliberations of its Syndicate, so, especially during several months in this year, he acted for the Vice-Chancellor during his absence, and was President of the Faculty of Arts. He also delivered on several occasions lectures to the Bethune Society on such subjects as the 'University of Cambridge,' the Employment of Women in Humane and Charitable Works.' This year his subject was 'The Clouds of Aristophanes,' in which he drew a lively picture of the great Grecian philosophic reformer Socrates, and the tremendous effect which he produced upon the old-fashioned superstition-mongers of Athens. The moral of this lecture, though it set forth very plainly the weakness of the old superstitions of India, was hardly brought out with sufficient clearness, and left the native young men who heard it in some doubt as to whether Socrates was meant tosymbolize the leader of the Brahmo Somaj movement or Dr. Duff.

Another effort for the benefit of the educated natives, and tending more directly towards their Christianization was the inauguration of six lectures to them in the Cathedral on "The Need, Evidence, and Difficulties of a Supernatural Revelation." They were delivered by the Bishop, Archdeacon Pratt, and four missionaries—two of the S. P. G., one of whom was the Rev. K. M. Banerjea, and two of the C. M. S. The audiences varied in the Cathedral from 300 to about 100. The lectures were afterwards delivered a second time in the hall of the Free Kirk Institution, at the request of the successor to Dr. Duff, and there the numbers rose to so large a figure as 800.

In the month of April the Bishop and Archdeacon Pratt paid a visit to the German Mission at Chotâ Nagpore, founded by Gössner, and bequeathed by him at his death to the care of two parent committees in Berlin. The mission was at a stand-still for want of funds, and it was at the request of the Commissioner of Chotá Nagpore and the chaplain of Hazareebaugh, in whose district it lay, that the chief authorities of the Indian Church went to see what could best be done for it. Three days were spent at Ranchi in the examination of the mission, and the Bishop returned to Calcutta deeply impressed with the reality and great importance of its work. He at once wrote to the Gössner Committee in Berlin, entreating that the impoverished condition of the mission might receive immediate attention, and alluded to the well-known dying wish of Gössner "that it might be received into the arms of the English Church" as a practicable solution of its difficulties. The Rev. Mr. Venn was also apprized that it was possible he might recieve overtures from the Berlin Committee, and if he did so was urged to accept them. It is of course now well-known that in the year 1868 the Berlin Committee sent out an Emissary who insisted on the original missionaries at Ranchi submitting to supersession and degradation or considering themselves no longer connected with the mission. The missionaries chose the latter alternative; their cause was taken up by a considerable majority of the native converts, numbering about 6,000, and pastors and flock were received together in 1869 under the auspices of the present Bishop of Calcutta into the arms of the S. P. G.

The summer of 1864, though thus marked by many items of important work, was in some respects the saddest period of the Bishop's Indian career. One cloud that marked it was the death, at Nynee-Tal, of his former Domestic Chaplain Mr. Burn, who had laboured with him, to use his own expression, "*as a son with a father*," during the earliest years of his episcopate. Another more continuous cloud was the absence of Mrs. Cotton in England, through ill-health, with their little girl. His letters to the latter are so exquisite of their kind that we cannot resist the pleasure of giving an extract from one of them belonging to this period. It is dated July 21st, 1864:—

"I have bad news for you to-day. Poor parrot is dead! I cannot make out why he died: certainly Maharaj took care of him and gave plenty of seed and water, and he always seemed to me very happy, till one day Maharaj observed that he was *bimār* (sick), and next morning when I went to see him, he was clinging to the lowest part of his perch, panting and very unhappy. That day he died. I have sent him to the Asiatic Society to be stuffed for you, so that you may again look at his pretty green back and red stomach; but he will never frighten aunt Julia again, or croak at us like a frog when we pass him in the verandah. I have your letter written on June 28th, when you were getting near Aden. I liked your letter very much, but I want to see you. O my pussy, my pussy, why don't you come and say 'night, night!' to Papa? * * * I shall want to know all you think of Granny, and brother Edward, and Hyde Park, and the Pantheon, and the gold fish, and the talking dolls, and every thing else that you see.

"*P.S.*—What do you think the cow has done? She and her calf were sent to feed in the cathedral close, and when the people went to bring them to their stall at night, where do you think they found them? Inside the cathedral!"

In the midst of the pelting rains of August, the Bishop left Calcutta with the view of entering upon his periodical visitation; but first as matters of importance required his presence at Simla, he proceeded direct to that place. One of these was the removal of the Bishop's school from Jutog, where it had first been established, four miles from the Simla Bazaar, and the Simla medical man, into the station of Simla itself. In the foundation and progress of this,

his '*first-born child*' so to speak among those Indian educational seminaries, with which his name as Bishop will always be chiefly connected, he had always displayed the warmest interest. He had alluded to it when he first broached the great subject of extended Anglo-Indian education at the thanksgiving service of 28th July 1860, on which occasion the large subsequent collection for the object was started by a donation from Lord and Lady Canning, of Rs. 11,000. It continued a prominent topic in his subsequent communications with the Indian Government, which evoked in October 1860 Lord Canning's memorable minute in favour of the Bishop's scheme for schools in the hills and plains, the renewal of the charter (as it has been called) of Anglo-Indian education.

In March 1863, he had been able to rejoice that it had been opened, and early in 1864 that it had a complement of 65 boys, the utmost number the buildings could receive. Thus to a certain extent all had been well, but experience had proved that the location of the school at such a distance from Simla was in every way a mistake; and it was in order to provide some plan for its removal, at the earliest possible opportunity, into a more central position, that the Bishop's presence was required. We cannot give the history of the matter better than in his own words—"I have been over to Jutog, and the chief thing which impressed me was the unfitness of the place for school. It is beautiful and healthy, *voila tout!* To carry on the school in three detached bungalows at considerable intervals, is fatal to discipline. The distance, too, from the doctor is serious. In the winter the solitude of the place is an objection. Jutog was pleasant to the eye, but has been tried and found wanting. Yet we have spent a large sum upon it; what must be done? At this juncture a *Deus ex machinâ* in the shape of the Supreme Government descends from the Empyrean, and announces a plan of establishing a military ophthalmic hospital, for which Jutog is well suited. Government will buy our bungalows for what they are worth, and, it is hoped, will find us a site in Simla too."

This then, in brief, was the history of the transference of the Bishop's school from Jutog to Knollwood, where it now stands. The unexpected opposition, however, of the Rajah to whom the ground at Knollwood belonged, and who was at last with difficulty propitiated by taking in exchange for it a village near Subathoo, delayed the carrying out of the plan till the year 1868.

The other point which called for the Bishop's presence at Simla was a petition which had been presented by some of the Government *employés* for the use of the Station Church at Simla for Presbyterian worship. Sir John Lawrence had received the petition, and had forwarded it to the Bishop, recommending it to his favourable consideration in consequence of the want of church accommodation at Simla. As a Presbyterian Church has now, we believe, been built at Simla, it is unnecessary to enter at any length into the phases which the controversy assumed. Suffice it to say that the Bishop declared himself unable to see any parallel between the wants of a Highland Regiment which, if not accommodated, might have had to broil in the open air under an Indian sun, and a few Presbyterians at a hill station occasionally visited by a Scotch minister on leave; and wrote so strongly to the Government against the scheme as likely to lead to confusion, difficulties and discontent, that they declined to press the plan, and leaving his letter unanswered, allowed the matter to drop. It is to be hoped that the course which the Bishop took in this case, will be remembered by any who may be apt to accuse him of latitudinarianism and want of church feeling.

In October, in company with his Domestic Chaplain, Mr. Cowie (now Bishop of Auckland in New Zealand), the Bishop quitted Simla, and proceeded by way of Dhurmsala and Dalhousie to Lahore. Forty-eight miles of the journey down the Ravee were performed by means of a conveyance which we will allow him to describe in his own words—"A charpoy bedstead is placed upon two large *mussucks*, each made from an entire buffalo's hide, and on this charpoy the traveller sits or lies. At the head and also at the foot of the charpoy is another *mussuck*, on which a man lies upon his stomach, grasping the charpoy with his hands and paddling in the water with his feet. We had five of these conveyances—one for me, one for Cowie, one for Shadrach with a little luggage, one for David with a little more, and the fifth for the remainder of the luggage. Hence you see that altogether twenty deceased buffaloes were needed for our conveyance. Thus we descended the river, and whenever I was in front and looked back at the advancing fleet, I was amused by watching the ten pairs of human legs moving up and down in the water like oars. Generally we floated along pleasantly enough; sometimes we were violently tossed up and down in a rapid, and sometimes the torrent was either so swift or the water so shallow that we had to get out and walk along the shingly shore. The drawbacks were two—when going through a rapid we were terribly splashed, once I was drenched to the skin, and latterly the sun was very hot."

The 48 miles were accomplished in 5½ hours, that is, at a rate of nearly nine miles an hour.

From Lahore the Bishop proceeded to Ferozepore where an especial subject of interest in his ministrations was the confirmation of 16 of the Muzhibi Sikhs in the presence of the Christians of the station and of their heathen comrades. There is nothing in his journey between Ferozepore and Calcutta that need particularly detain us. He notices with approval the Lombardic Brick Church at Bareilly 'rather heavy outside, but strikingly good within,' and says that it 'completes the attractiveness of the station.' He spent Christmas-day at Lucknow and reached Calcutta (still showing marks of the terrible cyclone of the 5th October 1864) early in 1865.

The most important events which occurred during his seven weeks' stay in Calcutta beyond the usual routine of confirmations, European and native, an ordination and a short missionary tour in the Krishnaghur district were—(1) the choral service at the cathedral (which was held for some years annually) on Shrove-Tuesday. Of this the Bishop says, after alluding to the numbers of the choir and the nature of the service, "I preached to a very large congregation including almost all the members of the Government; the Imperial Council having courteously adjourned that it might spend the morning in harmony instead of disputation." And (2) the opening of the Cathedral Mission College by the C. M. S. in a native house not far from their Amherst-street mission. After visiting it, the Bishop writes—"I trust that God's blessing may rest upon it: it realizes very completely some of my most cherished wishes,—the committal of the higher education of India to good earnest Christians, the union of secular and religious learning, the application of missionary efforts to the educated Bengalis, *the greater prominence of our own church in educational matters in Calcutta.*

Among the secular events witnessed by him at this period, the Bishop notices the review of the British troops intended for the expedition into Bhootan by the Governor-General Sir John Lawrence, the Commander-in-Chief Sir Hugh Rose, and the Duke of Brabant who happened to be on a valetudinarian visit to the East at the time.

Early in March his wife and daughter having returned from England, the Bishop's party quitted Calcutta and turned their faces to the far north-west. At Delhi he laid the foundation-stone of the S. P. G. Mutiny Memorial Church. Holy week and Easter were spent at Lahore. From thence it seems to have been his intention to proceed direct to Cashmere through the exclusively royal road of the Bunnihal Pass, but the Maharajah's favourite wife having died, and His Majesty being unable to do anything except cherish his inconsolable grief, the necessary leave could not be obtained and the longer route by Murree had to be adopted. So before the end of April the Bishop's party found themselves at Murree in temporary quarters awaiting the commencement of their expedition into the Vale of Cashmere.

On Tuesday, the 2nd May 1865, the Bishop's party, consisting of himself, Mrs. Cotton and their little girl, Mr. Hardy the newly arrived, and Mr. Cowie the retiring, Domestic Chaplain, who was about to enter on his duties as summer, chaplain at Srinaggar, left Murree and entered upon their journey into Cashmere. For twenty miles they travelled through British territory, and then crossing the rapid stream of the Jhelum they were landed amid stones and mud—fit emblems of the moral condition of the Cashmerians—in the Maharajah's territory. Eight days' march in dandis (a peculiar kind of litter, slung hammock-wise to a long straight bamboo) through a difficult country enriched with great variety of European flowering and fruit trees, Himalayan deodars, and grand pines, and presenting frequent views of the foaming Jhelum roaring along between its steep banks, brought them to Baramula where the valley begins.

Here there awaited them a long narrow barge with thirty-six rowers, eighteen in front and eighteen to the rear of a sort of raised dais, something like an enormous tea-tray covered with a red floor-cloth surmounted by a red canopy with curtains all around and seventeen other boats of ruder construction; so disposing of themselves and their *impedimenta*; upon these they voyaged up the stream, and on Friday, May 11th, entered Srinaggar ('holy city') of which the Jhelum forms the principal street, the houses being built on each side of it and coming flush down to the water with landing places at intervals. Having passed through the city, they landed and encamped upon the pleasant green board, planted with planes and poplars, along which some of the bungalows are situate, which have been built by the Maharajah for European visitors, having the *Takht-i-Suleiman* (Solomon's throne) a steep rocky hill rising about 1,000 feet from the valley just behind their camp. In a letter to his son giving an account of the place, the Bishop says:—'The English visitors here every summer are numerous; the young officers on leave amuse themselves by shooting (especially bears) and fishing, or rather spearing fish. This amusement is denied to the natives, at least in the neighbourhood of the city by the Maharajah, because his *guru* or spiritual preceptor, told him that his father's soul had migrated after death into a fish, and this fish might be killed. This we were told by one of the royal officials. 'But why,' we asked, 'is not the fish as liable to be killed by a European as by a Cashmerian? 'That,' replied our informant reverentially, 'God only can explain.'

The only missionary work which the Maharajah will tolerate in his dominions is the C. M. S. Medical Mission under the auspices of Dr. Elmsley who, with a praiseworthy self-devotion, has betaken himself summer after summer to this happy valley

Of nature so favored, of man so defiled,

to do what good he can to the bodies and souls of the unfortunate beings who swarm in the bazaars and purlieus of Srinaggar. To this mission the Bishop paid a visit, and after having seen a specimen of each day's work, the native catechist reading and expounding to the invalids a portion of the Sermon on the Mount, and the doctor himself, with his two young native Christian assistants, ministering the requisite remedies to each patient in succession, he writes—"Altogether considering the ignorance and wretchedness of the patients, and the entirely disinterested character of the mission, the scene appeared to me most interesting and edifying, and could not fail to remind me of Him who went about all Galilee, preaching the gospel of the kingdom and healing all manner of sickness and all manner of disease among the people."

The Bishop's stay at Srinaggar extended over a period of seventeen days. He consecrated a cemetery for Europeans, and took his share in the Sunday services at the Resident's house, and the intervals of time were chiefly spent in explorations of the beauties or antiquities of the surrounding neighbourhood, such as the splendid Siva-temples at Aventipura, (where he initiated an excavation which subsequently brought to light a long buried magnificent peristyle), the suntemples of Bhowan or Mâtân and Mortand, (Sancir Sun) and the Buddhist caves on the river Lidar. Before the end of May the return journey to Murree was commenced. The river route was adopted as far as Baramula, and from thence the journey was diversified by taking the right bank of the Jhelum; the Punjab was regained by crossing the light suspension bridge over the Mansuck, and the sanatarium of Murree was reached before the middle of June.

On arriving at his summer home, the Bishop laid out with his usual insatiable appetite for work, a very stiff course of study, and while pursuing it day by day continued also the correspondence necessary for the administration of his diocese and for the furtherance of his educational scheme. A part of that always was to occupy the Himalayas from west to east at intervals with a chain of schools which might act as the principal training places for the European and Eurasian children who lived in their neighbourhood. Among these Simla took the lead, and now after the Boys' school there had been established a Girls' school was added to it by transferring to Simla one which had been already set on foot at Dharamsala.

In the Eastern Himalayas an opportunity was found in 1864 for occupying Darjeeling with St. Paul's School which, through the severe competition it had met with in Calcutta from St. Xavier's College, the Doveton and La Martinière, was fast becoming bankrupt. Accordingly in that year the premises in Calcutta were sold to Government, a property was purchased in the best part of Darjeeling, a large school building capable of accommodating more than a hundred boys was commenced, and before many months had elapsed, the institution refreshed with a second youth had commenced that career which, when Darjeeling is brought into easier communication with Calcutta and the plains by the construction of a railway, can scarcely fail to be of the fairest as well as the most useful character.

In the Central Himalyas an excellent girls' school had been already established solely by the energy and untiring diligence of Archdeacon Pratt at Cainville House, Mussoorie; and in 1865 the Bishop began to see his way to adding to this a boys' school. The way to his plan was opened by the desire of Mr. Maddock, who had succeeded in establishing at Mussoorie a boys' school of excellent character, to retire from his post. By dint of great exertions on the part of the Bishop, the Archdeacon and the Diocesan Board, aided by Government, the payment of the purchase money Rs. 1,20,000 was provided for, and after some unavoidable delay the school passed in due course into the hands of the Diocese Board of Education.

In the case of each of these institutions, besides the provision of suitable buildings, the Bishop's scheme also embraced endowment funds, and for these both he and the Archdeacon strove untiringly, and happily with such success that now in every case the fate of all the schools may be pronounced to be, with careful management, secure.

In his summary of work accomplished at Murree during this summer, the Bishop puts down in addition to what we have already mentioned, an appeal to the shareholders for a 'Punjab and Delhi Railway Clergy Fund,' like that which by the Archdeacon's exertions was being gathered for the East Indian Railway. A weekly Sunday Sermon—Pastoral visits to the Lawrence Asylum and to Munkote, twelve miles from Murree—weekly lectures on three of the minor prophets—weekly meetings for reading the Bible at his house, attended regularly by some of the higher Government officials, aud subsequently a weekly Bible class with the soldiers of the convalescent depôt.

About the middle of October he commenced his visitation for the winter months by a trip into the Hazara district, attended by a guard and armed escort, and as a precaution against Mussulman fanatics and savage brigands. He subsequently proceeded to Attock, Peshawur, some of the stations towards Sind adjoining the Indus, Mooltan and Lahore. Christmas week was spent in the Hissar district, south of Delhi. From Agra he made an expedition to Muttra by Futtehpore, Sikri, Bhurtpore, and Deeg.

We need not dwell upon what he says of these last-named places which are all of the deepest historic interest, but we cannot refrain from giving our readers the benefit of the legend which accounts for the heat of Mooltan. "On approaching the tomb of Shamach Tabreez (Shamach—the sun of Beth Shemesh) we were told the reason of the excessive heat by the guardian of the shrine. Shamach Tabreez, he said, was a very holy *fakir* who came to Mooltan 250 years ago, but the people refused to receive him, or to listen to his preaching, desired him to leave their city, and declined to supply him with any kind of food. A disciple, however, brought him some game from the jungle, and he begged from the churlish Mooltanese fire wherewith to cook it. This they also refused. Whereupon the *fakir* said that if they would not help him to cook his food, the sun should do so; and accordingly, by his prayers, brought the sun near enough to Mooltan to provide him with an excellent roast hare. Once there, however, the sun declined to return to his former place in the heavens, and so the people of Mooltan are still punished for the impiety of their ancestors by an extra allowance of heat."

The Bishop's palace was reached early in February 1866.

The Bishop never appeared in more thoroughly working trim than when he was returning from Upper India to '*those pleasant plains*' (as he playfully termed them) in February 1866. We had at this time the privilege, during the temporary absence of his Domestic Chaplain, of meeting him at Chinsurah, where he preached for the Additional Clergy Society, and held a Confirmation on Tuesday, February 4th, and of accompanying him thence to Calcutta, and well do we remember the cheerfulness, the ardour, and the interest with which he talked over the condition and progress of all the educational and charitable institutions of the city regarding which we had any information to offer.

The authorities of the Doveton College in the midst of the difficulties with which they had been for some time beset, and which they only avoided by trenching on capital funds had sought his counsel and advice, and even asked him to take upon himself the office of their *Visitor.* This he had consented to do upon the condition 'of their allowing church-teaching and catechising for any of their pupils who wished for it, at the hand of the chaplains of St. John's, and accordingly as a public sign of his acceptance of the Visitorship he took the chair on Thursday, 1st March, at their annual general meeting, and delivered an address full of pithy remarks and practical suggestions on the nature and mode of proper school management, and the evils of a system of education which for show's sake crammed the few at the expense of the many—a process which he compared to that of the gardener who, in order to get a few fat prize gooseberries, stripped the rest of the tree, and concentrated all his attention upon the half-dozen which through their extraordinary dimensions were to puff him into credit and renown.

On Easter-Eve, 31st March, the Bishop attended the final debate in the Supreme Council upon the Native Converts' Re-marriage Bill, a subject which had caused him considerable anxiety and discomfort in consequence of a divergence of opinion upon it between himself and a considerable body of his clergy, among whom was Archdeacon Pratt. The object of the Bill was to allow a native Christian, whose wife, after his conversion, was not willing to live with him, to be legally absolved from wedlock, and to be at liberty to marry again. We cannot here enter into all the niceties of the controversy which was discussed for several successive months in the pages of the *Christian Intelligencer*, formed the subject of debate at several clerical meetings at the Palace, and was submitted to all the Church of England chaplains and missionary clergy in India for their opinion, but in general terms we may say that the Bishop was decidedly in favour of the Bill, contending that simple desertion, if persisted in, constituted according to St. Paul (1 Cor. vii. 15.) a proper ground of divorce.

The other side argued that it was not necessary to suppose that St. Paul contemplated re-marriage in the case in question, that judging from experience the wife, if patiently waited for, invariably in the end rejoined her husband, that there was no proper reason for divorce except that stated in the Sermon on the Mount (Mat. v. 32), and that a virtuous wife, if she continued a heathen, was under no condition that justified her husband in casting her off and marrying another. The Bill eventually became Law, and perhaps, as a matter of state-craft, it may be justified; for in point of fact since the passing of Mr. Anderson's Marriage Act in 1864, which laid down as a condition of the validity of marriages between Christians, that no husband or wife should be living, various native converts had been united in wedlock in an illegal manner. It may be doubted, however, whether there was any necessity for the Bishop's being so strenuous a supporter as he was of a measure which at the best can only be regarded as a concession to men because of the hardness of their hearts.

On the 31st May in this summer, the Bishop and Mrs. Cotton inaugurated those large evening gatherings at the Palace which have done so much to encourage kindly feeling among the various classes of society in Calcutta, and especially to bring the native gentry (and their wives also in some cases) into friendly intercourse with Europeans. The whole first floor of the Palace was thrown open for an 'At Home,' and from 9 till near midnight the drawing-room, the spacious library, and the extensive verandahs were alive with a busy crowd, bent only upon making themselves mutually agreeable and upon learning how to appreciate and understand each other better than they had done before.

On the morning of May 31, 1866, an event had taken place of considerable significance to the ecclesiastical world of India. The large library of Dr. Kay, the late Principal of Bishop's College, was sold by public auction. This was an outward sign that he had permanently retired from the post which ill-health had obliged him personally to leave two years before, and it may serve as an introduction to a few words upon Bishop Cotton's ideas of the usefulness of the college and of the plans which he proposed for increasing its efficiency. The S. P. G. at home, wearied with the constant expense to which the college put them, and the small comparative fruit which it appeared to bear, had been occupied in sifting its estate and condition in a series of special sub-committees, and seemed bent upon some drastic measure which might either abolish it altogether as an incumbrance, or else entirely alter the aspect which it had gradually assumed. The Bishop did not deny that it had considerably fallen short of the high hopes of its venerable founder, and especially so in the matter of acting as a nursery and training place for the native pastorate of the whole Indian peninsula; but the founder had not foreseen that native pastors might be better trained nearer their own homes and in places where their own tongue was spoken than in the moist and relaxing climate of Lower Bengal which was to them as a foreign land. Considerations of this kind reduced the field from which the native pastor element in Bishop's College, could be drawn with advantage to the S. P. G. missions in the Sunderbuns, which, after all, would yield but a small harvest.

The East Indians, who had chiefly benefited by the advantages the college had to offer, had not, it might be allowed, justified the hopes that were entertained of them; but still it was unchristian to despair of a whole race, because of the misdemeanours of a few of them. The College, as it stood, supplied a want which, if its constitution were materially altered, or the quality of its staff reduced, would soon be severely felt; for it was the only suitable training-place which the Diocese possessed for theological attainments of any thing like a high order. Its press, moreover, had not been unfruitful in the production of valuable translations into the Vernacular, as well as standard works in English, of considerable merit. The college, therefore, was doing a good and valuable, though not perhaps showy, work, and the best plan to increase its efficiency would be to make it thoroughly Diocesan, and by abandoning the plan of home management to throw it more upon its own responsibility and resources, to which end a good large special fund should be raised by way of endowment. In the meantime the best thing to be done was to send out with all possible speed an energetic and enterprising principal, who would in a few months be better able to advise upon a profitable course of action than half a hundred sub-committees sitting in London. The health of the excellent Acting Principal (the Rev. T. Skelton) entirely gave way in the second year of his tenure of office, so that he was obliged to go home on sick leave. After about a year's absence he returned to his post as Principal, but only to quit it in 1870, still more seriously out of health.

The situation, therefore, remains at present, in 1871, very much what it was when Bishop Cotton wrote home in 1866. As a training place for the native pastorate, the college never can, from the circumstances of its situation, draw from a large field with advantage, and so be conspicuously successful—the collection, which Bishop Cotton proposed of a new Endowment Fund with the view of rendering the college an independent diocesan institution, seems to be almost impossible, so long as its state and aims remain what they have been.

It remains as the best course to be pursued that the wise suggestions of Bishop Cotton who so thoroughly understood the missionary requirements and capabilities of his Diocese, and who was such an acknowledged master of the whole educational question in India, should be taken into very careful consideration before any sweeping change is made in the constitution of the college or the form which it has gradually assumed, altered in any material degree.

A measure of considerable importance to the Indian Ecclesiastical Establishment regarding which correspondence had been going on with the Home Government for some years previously, was consummated in the year 1866. The two Senior Chaplaincies, which had been, from the higher allowances that they brought with them, the great prizes of the service, were abolished, and the money saved to Government thereby was expended upon raising the amount of the Chaplains' retiring pensions. Since 1834, they had stood at £292 per annum. They were now by this scheme raised to their old figure of £365. The three Indian Bishops when they met at Bombay in 1863 had all concurred in signing in favor of the scheme. One of its results will doubtless be the conducing to earlier retirement on the part of Chaplains, and the introduction of a fresher and more vigorous element into the ranks of the service—a point which Bishop Cotton considered of such vital importance, that, at his special suggestion, a clause was added to the scheme rendering retirement after 25 years of service compulsory.

We now proceed, before passing to the final tour of the Bishop into Assam, during the course of which his valuable life was brought to such a sudden and lamentable close, to gather up a few items of information from his correspondence about this time.

He was always fully alive to the importance of an increase of the episcopate in the north of India, and at various periods he had sketched out plans to that end, by means of voluntary effort seconded by Government approval and sanction; but he deprecated most earnestly any premature disturbances of the system of the Indian dioceses, or reduction of them to the ordinary Colonial level, as will appear by the following extract from a letter written to the Bishop of London during the spring of 1866 :—

"I have been disturbed by a letter just received from Mr. Venn of the Church Missionary Society, in which he says that though the Bill just brought into the House of Commons by Government to decide about the status of Colonial Bishops does not refer to India, yet the lawyers think that it will over-ride the acts on which the Indian Patent rests. I wish to say very earnestly that in my opinion the principles on which the status of Colonial Bishops may be settled are at present altogether inapplicable, and that I should esteem it a serious and quite peculiar misfortune for the Church here if anything were done to unsettle its connexion with the Crown and Church of England.

"It should be remembered that our Church in this country is in a state of transition, and that it would be quite premature to attempt to fix at present its permanent condition. We are a small Christian body in a heathen country, and the majority of Englishmen in India have no intention of remaining here permanently. These two facts are alone sufficient to show that the Church in India is in an entirely different position from the Church in a settled colony with a fixed Christian population."

In reply to a letter from the Bishop of Cape Town, inviting him to the Lambeth Pan-Anglican Conference, and stating that in his charge of 1863 he had expressed himself in favour of some General Assembly representing the Church of England in its various branches and provinces, he wrote (22nd May 1866) saying, that he contemplated a Synod meeting under the control of the English Monarchy and Parliament, and not an assembly which, however much entitled to moral weight, had no power to enforce its decrees, and that he doubted whether it were worth while for such a mere voluntary Conference to take so strong a step as to summon all the

Colonial Bishops from all points of the world to London; but however that might be, the terms of his appointment absolutely precluded him from the possibility of attending, as no power on earth could enable him to go to England before November 1868 except an Act of Parliament, or the visitation of so formidable an illness that his medical attendant would be able to certify that he could not safely continue in India.

Allusion is found in a letter to his son, dated May 27th, to the terrible famine in Orissa, Krisnaghar and other districts of Lower Bengal, and to the subscription commenced for its alleviation; and in another letter dated July 1866, to the failure of the Agra Bank; but we must pass over these in company with other minor matters and hasten to the concluding scene.

The expedition into Assam formed part of the regular scheme of Diocesan Visitation, and was taken up in the rains as the most propitious period for travelling in that roadless region, where the best and safest, and, in many instances, the only highways are the natural water-courses. It was commenced on the 1st of August. The party proceeded to Kooshtea by rail and there embarked in the flat *Rhotas* (the same as had been used in 1849 for the voyage up the Ganges) in tow of the Government steamer *Koel.* It consisted of the Bishop and Mrs. Cotton, Mr. Woodrow, School Inspector, and Mrs. Woodrow, Dr. Powell and Mr. Vallings, Diocesan Secretary, S. P. G., who officiated as Domestic Chaplain; Mr. Hardy being detained in Calcutta through illness. An untoward event happened at the outset of the voyage, which seemed afterwards a sort of dim foreshadowing of its mournful close. On the first Saturday, the very *same day of the week* as that on which the Bishop was drowned, just also after a *religious service* and in the dark of the *advancing night*, evening prayers being ended on board at 10 P.M. the cry was raised of a man overboard. One of Mr. Woodrow's servants sleeping on the edge of the deck of the steamer had rolled over unconsciously and fallen into the water. A buoy was thrown out and a boat let down immediately, but *the man was never seen again.*

The voyage and the visitation of the various stations in Assam occupied about a month. The interesting S. P. G. Mission at Tezpore under Mr. Hesselmeyer, the primitive station of Seebsaugor, where for lack of servants all the ladies had to act *ayahs* on their own account, where no bread or wine was procurable for the administration of the Sacrament, and where the opium godown had to be indented upon for the supply of furniture for the Church service; Dibroghur, where the pretty Church was consecrated under the name of St. Paul's, and whither some of the native Christians from Ranchi had found their way as coolies upon one of the tea estates, together with various other stations such as Goalpara, Gowhatti, Jeypore, Nazeerah, Nowgong, were all of them looked up, and by the 9th September the Bishop, on his return voyage, was at Dacca. In his diary at this place he remarks: "On the whole, we of the English Church have reason to be ashamed of our position at Dacca, the fragments of Hæberlin's mission which existed in 1861, have now vanished: the chaplains here have done nothing to keep it together, and every thing has passed into the hands of the Baptists. Next to Calcutta there is no place in Bengal where education has made so much progress as at Dacca; for, besides the college, there are several good aided schools, and a large body of Brahmoists is forming in consequence. *The fields seem white to harvest, but we Anglicans are doing nothing to gather in the crop.*"

From Dacca an excursion was made to Sylhet and Cherrapoonjee on the Kossyah Hills where "a whiff of mountain air upon the fresh open and invigorating country" did something towards dispelling the attacks of Assam fever from which the Bishop had been suffering more or less during the whole of his journey. From Shillong he wrote a letter to his mother-in-law, Mrs. Tomkinson, full of plans for the return of her daughter to England in 1868, and of anticipations of his re-joining her there about the end of that year.

Dacca was again reached on Wednesday, 3rd October, and the whole party once more assembled on board the *Rhotas* departing for Kooshtea. The closing scene cannot be given better than in Mrs. Cotton's own words :—

The Bishop had a fresh touch of the fever which he invariably caught during any protracted sojourn among river damps. "On Saturday October 6th, he got up far from well; but he mended as the day wore on, and had a long conversation in the forenoon with Mr. Woodrow on some school matters. The vessels were anchored at Kooshtea by midday when the party broke up, some proceeding at once by train to Calcutta; the Bishop and myself remained on board for the evening work. The Bishop ate his luncheon and appeared decidedly better. Between 3 and 4, when lying on sofa in the pleasant sitting room of the *Rhotas*, he said suddenly 'Shut all the windows.' They were open to let in the cool air for the day was cloudy and pleasant. His hands were very cold and a fresh fever fit seemed coming on, but some strong hot tea revived him and at 5 o'clock he left the boat for the consecration of the cemetery, feeling not otherwise than equal to the exertion. He expected to return by seven, dine and leave by the night train. At the service of the consecration he gave, as was his wont, a short extempore address * * He reminded his hearers "that such consecrations were for the benefit of the living not of the dead; that departed souls suffered no injury if their bodies were left in a desert place or on a field of battle or in any other way were unable to receive the rites of burial; that the solemn ceremony of consecration was to enable the living in a better manner to pay the last tribute of affection, and to retain a more solemn and permanent impression of the awful truths which gave eternal importance to the questions of life and death." After the service was over, he lingered to discuss some ecclesiastical arrangements with the very few residents of the small station, and twilight was fast passing into darkness when he reached the river-bank. Owing to currents, churs (sandbanks) and the precipitous nature of the bank, it was impossible to bring any vessel up close. The *Rhotas* was lying in the full stream; an intervening flat was between it and the shore, and this flat the Bishop prepared to reach. But between himself and all to which he was looking forward as perhaps still to be permitted to him in this world, unfinished work and fresh formed plans, active labour yet for a space in India, dawning hopes of England and English friends—between himself and all except the Master he had striven faithfully to serve there lay many yards of the rapidly rolling river.* Somewhere on the perilous causeway of planks bridging the waters his foot slipped, he fell, and was never more seen. The increasing darkness, and unsteady platform,

* It should be understood that a safer but more circuitous route to the shore had been provided by means of passing from the *Rhotas* to the steamer and so to the bank higher up. The way the Bishop took was intended for the native coolies only, being the shortest.

his near sight, the weariness of a frame enfeebled for the time by fever, had doubtless a share, humanly speaking, in the great calamity foreknown in the counsels of Him who moves in a mysterious way! Every effort was made to rescue, to recover him. All who are acquainted with the current of an Indian river, well know how infinitely slight would be the chance of success in the one endeavour or the other.

There were those to whose lips, on hearing the mournful tidings the simple Bible words arose :—*And Enoch walked with God and he was not, for God took him.*"

The news of the accident was communicated by telegraph from Kooshtea to Calcutta in the early morning hours of Sunday, the 7th October 1866. His Domestic Chaplain Mr. Hardy had proceeded to the Railway Station to meet him, and on the platform at Sealdah the telegram was placed in his hands announcing that the Bishop was no more. The sad intelligence, of course, spread rapidly through the town, and was received in every quarter—among Europeans, Eurasians and Natives alike—with the most profound concern and sorrow.

Just when he had gained the confidence and affection of all classes—just when he had become thoroughly acquainted with India and its wants—and, just when his powers were at their best to minister to them, he had been snatched by the merest momentary *accident* from his post of such extended and varied usefulness.

The Bishop had left a clause in his will requesting that if he died in Calcutta his mortal remains might repose side-by-side with Bishop Wilson's in the Cathedral vault. In case Government objected to this intramural interment, he desired that his body might be laid in the Military burial-ground at Alipore, seeing that he himself was the son of an officer, and that his only son had lately become an officer in the Royal Artillery. All efforts, however, to recover his body from the river in which it had sunk proved entirely fruitless. His very hat, and the stick with which he was feeling his way across the planks, sank with him into the stream and never were seen again. A reward of Rs. 2,000 was offered in the name of Government for the recovery of his remains. After a few days, a telegram arrived to say that some natives had appeared claiming the reward for finding them, and preparations were commenced for their interment in the Cathedral.

It was thought necessary, however, in the first instance, to ensure that the reward was not being claimed under false pretences, and upon a commission proceeding from Calcutta to the spot to identify the body, it was found to be that of a native which the stream had washed ashore a few miles below Kooshtea. Thus all opportunities of a demonstration of public regard in the form of a solemn interment in the Cathedral were lost, and the only means of testifying to the high estimation in which the Bishop was held was by letters of condolence with his widow, which poured in thickly from every quarter in the shape of extracts from the minutes of the Supreme Council, of the Calcutta University, of the Bethune Society, of the various Missionary Societies, Church and Dissenting alike, and especially of various strictly native societies who vied with the Europeans and Eurasians in doing honour to the memory of the deceased.

The first monument that was erected to his memory was a large mural brass which was affixed to the eastern walls of St. John's Church, Calcutta, the old Cathedral, at the cost of the Select Vestry. Subsequently a collection was made from the clergy throughout the diocese towards a tablet to be placed adjoining the reredos of the Cathedral, but it was felt on all hands that the most suitable monument to his memory was the subscription to his Hills and Plains School scheme which had yet two years to run before it was complete. To this great work, therefore, Archdeacon Pratt applied himself by at once issuing a circular upon the subject, and it was mainly through his untiring devotion and energy that the scheme was eventually brought to its fair and successful issue.

It was a saying of Bishop Cotton's that "the succession of the Calcutta Episcopate presented a roll of names to which any man might justly be proud to belong," and that each of them had left works behind him for the benefit of the diocese or of the world at large which never would lose their effect." And certainly the addition of his name to the series did not in any way tend to invalidate the truth of the affirmation, for we may safely say that the name of *Cotton's Schools* will last as long as Christian education subsists in India. Of all his predecessors, perhaps in powers, of conciliation and widespread general influence, he most resembled Heber, though in fire of genius and brilliancy of outward conversation, he undoubtedly fell far short of him.

To his immediate predecessor, Wilson, he presented in many respects a most striking contrast. Wilson's mind was narrow but deep, and his fervid feelings followed between the high banks of his lofty character with the force and rapidity of a mountain torrent carrying all obstacles before it as it dashes through its rocks to the plain. Cotton's mind resembled the same stream when it has reached a quieter and more even level. It was broader and less impulsive, moving on towards its object with less apparent effort, but still with a persistent will, which in the end accomplished what it had in view. The extreme caution which Cotton invariably displayed, his great anxiety to avoid giving offence, and his desire that his schemes should, as much as was possible, satisfy all parties and wound the feelings of no one, have been looked upon by some persons as sources of weakness in him and attributed to a lack of courage in his character; but still, as we have seen, when it was necessary to make a stand, he invariably did so and spoke in very decided and unmistakeable terms.

If there was one thing more than another which he thoroughly and cordially detested, it was religious partisanship, and the hollow, despicable cant with which it walls itself round while it eats out the very life and soul of Christianity. To any clergyman, high or low, who was endeavouring, according to his light, to save souls by a patient and laborious discharge of his duty, he was always a considerate adviser and a kind friend. In this sense he was a Broad Churchman, but by no means in the sense of tampering with any of the vital doctrines of Christianity, such as the divinity and all perfect sacrificial offering of our Blessed Redeemer, upon which point when once attacked in print with the covert insinuation "*We hope that our Diocesan believes in the Incarnation,*" he immediately wrote to defend himself with a warmth and an indignation quite unusual with him.

Among the benefits conferred by Bishop Cotton upon the ecclesiastical service, we may mention, in addition to the increase of pension to the chaplains, to which we have above alluded, a vastly improved code of rules for privilege leave, the establishment of certain staff appointments at large stations as a reward for meritorious service, certain promotion to the grade of senior chaplain after ten years' service, and the scheme which has already been carried out, though but to a very partial extent, of building a parsonage in connexion with every church in the Diocese.

The general estimation in which Bishop Cotton was held is shown by the following words which are taken from an *In Memoriam* in the *Bengal Hurkaru* :—" A scholar of vast and varied attainments—a divine whose profound conviction of the truth he professed was free from the very faintest trace of the illiberality and bigotry which have done so much to disfigure the glorious cause to which he devoted himself—a prelate whose overflowing charity, genial sympathy, and ever ready advice have strengthened the hands and encouraged the faltering hearts of numbers—a Christian whose humility made him accessible to the poorest, and whose severely consistent walk and wakeful self-denial made him an example to every class,—Dr. Cotton occupied a place in India which we are persuaded it will be exceedingly difficult to fill."*

* From a lecture on the Episcopate of Bishop Cotton, by the Revd. W. Spencer, Bengal Chaplain.

THE END.